Don't Stop the Music

DON'T STOP
THE
MUSIC

Robert Perske

Abingdon Press
Nashville

DON'T STOP THE MUSIC

Copyright © 1986 by Robert Perske

This book is printed on acid-free paper.

BOOK DESIGN BY JOHN ROBINSON

Library of Congress Cataloging-in-Publication Data

PERSKE, ROBERT.
 Don't stop the music.
 Summary: A journalist becomes involved with two young people
afflicted with cerebral palsy.
 [1. Cerebral palsy—Fiction. 2. Physically handicapped—Fiction.]
I. Title.
PZ7.P437Do   1986   [Fic]   86-17426

ISBN 0-687-11060-2 (soft: alk. paper)

MANUFACTURED BY THE PARTHENON PRESS AT
NASHVILLE, TENNESSEE, UNITED STATES OF AMERICA

For
Anne McDonald
and
Robert Williams

WHEN MY RUNNING FEET REACHED BLOCK FIFTEEN,

1

I caught my first glimpse of Long Island Sound. I lowered my head and leaned forward, my feet moved faster, and the slap-slapping of my shoes became louder. When I reached the beach, even the sand failed to slow my pace. I veered to the right and took that good old path to the grassy top of Lookout Ledge. I stopped at the edge and let nature take charge—the clean smell of sea air, the warmth of the rising sun on my face and, stretching beneath me, the vast expanse of blue water. I had grown up loving this spot. Coming back after being away always touched off a carnival inside me—confetti and waving flags and a sense of being home and free again.

Even the two strangers who had rattled me as I was running through Block Five were behind me now—or so I thought.

It was 6:14 A.M. on July 2. I had arrived at

Kennedy International yesterday morning after an exhausting two months in Australia. Now I, Barnaby Shane, was liberated from agents and editors until the day after Labor Day, free for the first time in three years to write whatever *I* wanted. Even the atmosphere made me feel that if I were a frisbee, I could sail off this ledge on the Connecticut shore and land on Long Island, ten miles away.

But enough of this, I said. I turned and began my fifteen-block return—back up Soundview Avenue, across Interstate 95, over the four New York to Boston railroad tracks, and up Throttle Hill another thirty feet to my grey bungalow with the white shutters. Once inside, I would need only minutes to shed my favorite purple-with-the-white-stripe running shorts and shirt, shower, and get into jeans and T-shirt. Grabbing coffee and a doughnut, I would head for the bedroom I used for an office and my word processor.

But as I approached Block Five again, thoughts of those strangers returned. On my run toward the beach, I had spied something different in that neighborhood. One house now had a wooden ramp which stretched the five yards from the sidewalk to the porch. The house was directly across from Soundview High School. On the porch, two people —both about sixteen—had been sitting in motorized wheelchairs, watching me like soldiers on lookout.

I recalled that, at my first full glimpse of the young man, I had said to myself, holy mackerel, the guy looks like me. He seemed shorter than my six feet, and I could tell from the way his jeans and T-shirt fit that he hadn't an ounce of fat. I was a little chubbier. His sandy hair was the color of mine and fashioned into the same efficient "mop top." He had the same sprinkling of freckles, and his eyes were brown like mine, too. The guy could have been my little brother.

The young woman, also in jeans and yellow T-shirt, was Charlie Brown's friend Lucy come to life. But unlike the *Peanuts* character, she was lovely, with delicate features and black silky hair. Eyes almost as dark as her hair had focused intensely on me as I came closer. She looked both dead serious and perky.

The young couple attracted me in some indescribable way. But seeing them in wheel-chairs had left me momentarily at a loss for words. I ran past them, felt uncomfortable about not speaking, turned and ran backward a few steps.

"Hi there," I said. "You two are up early."

As soon as they heard me, their arms flew out and upward as though they were attached to puppet strings, then circled as if trying to catch a whirling fly. Their heads bobbed like corks and they broke into wide-mouthed, wet grins, some of the water flowing over their chins. Their uncoordinated body movements caught me by surprise. Nevertheless, I had continued to backpedal, waiting for them to answer. When they didn't, I turned and moved on.

As I jogged away, I had tried to figure out why they bothered me. After all, I had been around more than my share of people with different life-styles. And I wasn't one of those mindless there-go-I-but-for-the-grace-of-Goders, either. Or at least I thought I wasn't.

And yet, there I was, on this first full day at home, running down the street, feeling as free as the wind, a flawless, well-tuned, precision human being, thighs lifting properly, arms swinging to the cadence of my feet, muscles flexing and relaxing perfectly. Then I had spied those two imprisoned ones—people with no speech, out-of-control muscles, probably mental retardation, all lumped together in wheelchairs. Those differences bothered me.

Then it struck me that I had felt this kind of uneasiness a few weeks earlier when an Aussie journalist friend tried to bend my ear and pour into it his coverage of a woman with severe disabilities in a celebrated Supreme Court case. When he started to describe her, I excused myself and said I had to get back to organizing my notes on the Gordon River Gorge.

"Give me your newsclips on the woman," I had said. "I'll read them later." The next day he gave me a manila envelope containing the stories. I had tucked it in the back of my suitcase—not unlike the way I had shoved to the back of my mind thoughts about the couple in the wheelchairs. Now, as I drew closer to Block Five, I wondered if the two strangers would still be on the porch.

They were.

Coming closer, I tried to think of something courteous to say. Then I noticed that the sun had just risen above the school across the street, brightening their porch.

"Hello again," I called ahead. "I'll bet that sun feels good."

My greeting apparently served as a signal. Immediately, the young man leaned forward and whirred his chair down the ramp. He stopped at the sidewalk's edge and awaited my approach.

Again, I felt flustered. I decided to keep up the pace, say something else nice and pass him on the run.

Then the young woman sped down the ramp, her left hand clutching a control on the armrest, her right arm flailing like a buckingbronc rider. She was so busy watching me, she rammed into the young man's chair, sending it into my path. I crashed into it, went into a flying somersault and landed on my back.

When I recovered my breath, I tried to rub the throbbing pain from my thighs, which had struck the armrest. Then the pain, my wounded ego, and the thought of their recklessness made me irrational—like a motorist who had just had his car smashed by someone running a stop sign.

"What's the matter with you two?" I shouted. "Don't you have any brains?"

I looked up, right into their eyes, in my interviewer's habit of trying to figure people out, sense things they couldn't put into words. I really expected two pair staring blankly into space as if all the forces behind them were out to lunch.

I couldn't have been more wrong.

By the time I zeroed in on them, four dark eyes were boring in on me. I saw steady, dignified, intelligent eyes . . . questioning eyes trying to figure *me* out . . . eyes that longed . . . eyes that made me feel shame and look away.

This flawless, well-tuned precision human being got up and tried once again to move down the street as free as the wind—trying desperately not to show a limp.

WHEN I WAS HOME,

2

the warm water of the shower took some of the kinks out of my legs; I would have a lingering soreness but no major injuries. I breathed a sigh of relief and sat down at my word processor with my doughnut and coffee.

But as my pain subsided, guilt began to gnaw. I knew by their eyes I had hurt them. Well, Barnaby Shane, I said, you messed up. But forget it for now. Get to work.

But my forgetter failed to function.

By 12:30, several cups of coffee had disappeared, my T-shirt was soaked with sweat, and my head ached. For five hours my fingers had rapped out sentences that soared like manhole covers. I rewrote them, rewrote them again, then canceled them off the screen. Over and over. It was as if two pair of dark eyes were looking over my shoulder, studying every phrase.

In an attempt to escape, I leaned back in my chair and let my mind recall the previous day.

☆   ☆   ☆

I had arrived at Kennedy International at 8:05 A.M., stepping from the 747 with a spring. My free-lance article for *The Smithsonian* was done and had been accepted for publication in October.

And something else quickened my step. I spied Mindy Guthrie, my free-lance writer friend, in slacks and a perky white blouse, waiting for me at the end of the ramp. Usually I took the airport limo, but we hadn't seen each other for some time, so she had driven down in my car. My heart melted as I moved toward that shapely little person with the bouncy chestnut hair. I felt even better when I got close enough to wrap her in my arms, smell her perfume, look closely into her pixielike face. Her soft blue eyes gave me a happy hello.

"You've had a feather cut," I said.

"Just for you," Mindy said. "Like it?"

"It's lovely," I said.

I could tell from her satisfied smile that I'd said what she wanted to hear. Then she stood back and surveyed me with concern.

"Are you tired, Barnaby?"

"Nope. The plane wasn't full, so I pushed up three armrests in the middle section and slept most of the way."

"Tell me all about it in the car."

"Okay, but you drive."

Mindy pulled out onto the Van Wyck Expressway, past Shea Stadium and over the Whitestone Bridge. Then she turned onto I-95 for the twenty-mile drive up the Connecticut side of Long Island Sound. While she drove, I spoke with machine-gun rapidity about the interesting people I'd met "down under" and how good it felt to be home again.

"How's the article?" Mindy interrupted after she had gotten her fill of my monologue.

"Finished," I said. "It's so great you could put it to music."

"You sound cocky."

"I am," I said. "No agents or editors to complicate my life until September. By the way, when do you leave for the Falklands?"

"Tonight at six. I'll be back on Labor Day."

"Good."

Mindy's eyes narrowed\and she looked at me from their corners until she saw my devilish smile.

"You don't want *me* to complicate your life, either," she said.

"Today, yes. Tomorrow, no."

"I feel the same way about you, Mr. Shane."

15

"More than me," I said. "You with that Katherine Hepburn syndrome, that stuff about not wanting to marry because your career involvements wouldn't be fair to your spouse."

"Come on. That's just Katie. I'll marry you someday, but my agent says I'm a promising writer, and I'm going to fulfill some of that promise first."

"You've already done it. Time and time again."

"Not as much as I want."

"Well, for gosh sakes. How much is . . . " I stopped without finishing the sentence. We had bled over this jagged issue many times during the last eight years. And though both of us had reached thirty-six, it remained an open wound. Knowing that my next response could spoil a lovely day, I clammed up.

Mindy's soft hand moved over mine, interlaced fingers and squeezed. We rode in silence for a while. When it seemed safe, she opened up again.

"I suppose you'll spend your free time working on that David-and-Goliath fetish of yours—little people networking to make a better world."

"Tomorrow," I acknowledged. "Got some new illustrations from watching all those unrepeatable Aussies. Did you know the

16

Australian government decided not to dam the Gordon River Gorge in Tasmania, which would have destroyed millions of acres of the country's most beautiful land? That decision cost the country a multimillion-dollar hydroelectric industry. And who made the government so responsive? A few handfuls of networking citizens. It was just like that handful of citizens who influenced our government to stop building the supersonic transport. You see, the SST was . . ."

Mindy rolled her eyes upward.

"What's the matter?"

"You just began your 405th sermon on little people and the SST."

"Sorry."

"Don't be. One of the things that makes me love you so much is your belief that ordinary people can play a large part in making society decent. Big business and government believe they're the only ones who do solid thinking. Your point of view is refreshing. Just get it on paper. You hear?"

"I'm going to try," I said.

When we reached the Throttle Hill exit, Mindy took the ramp up to Soundview Avenue, turned left to cross the highway and train overpasses, and prepared to turn left again into my driveway.

"Wait," I said. "Go around the square first."

17

Mindy turned right onto Front Street, a road that began in front of my place and ran parallel to the tracks. Like Rip Van Winkle, I studied everything with wide eyes. On the left was Throttle Hill Square, that block-long expanse of lush green grass I could see so vividly from my hilltop writing-room window. On the other side was our community postoffice, O'Rourke's News and Magazine Shop, a walkway leading to the commuter train platforms, and Vittorio's, my favorite diner. When Mindy turned left at the far end, I studied the next line of shops facing the green—McDonald's, Hankin's Hardware, Save-a-Lot Supermarket, Perkins' Drugstore, and the Immigrant's Trust Bank with its corner sign flashing the time and temperature in large cherry-red numbers. When we neared the bank, I looked back diagonally across the square at my place on the highest point of the hill. Then we traversed the last two sides.

Mindy sensed my pensiveness. "You love coming home, don't you, Barnaby?"

"Mindy, I do. I really do."

I opened my door to a happy surprise. Mindy had cleaned the house. No small task, considering the way I had left it. The table was set for a midday candlelight brunch.

Mindy busied herself in the kitchen while I checked the ancient pipes, the wiring, the tricky roof, and tempermental water heater. I moved through the routine just as my father had done for as long as I could remember before he and Mom relocated to Tucson and left the place for me.

As I entered the kitchen, I heard the diesel engines of a Boston-bound train move into lower gear and rev to a crescendo, getting louder and louder. Then, just as I'd seen Dad do to Mom, I grabbed Mindy.

"Hang on," I shouted. "The train sounds like it's going to jump the track." Mindy went along with my game as the noisy monster's whistle let out a scream like a soprano with her clothes on fire. Then as it gained speed and moved away, the tone dropped until it sounded like a baritone falling off a cliff. Windows rattled and dishes chattered. Mindy placed her soft cheek on my chest, hung on tightly, and didn't move until the train was at least twenty miles down the track.

After a lovely day of walking, talking, and caring, we suddenly noticed it was 4:10 P.M. We gave each other pained glances. Without talking, I drove Mindy to her apartment across town and loaded her suitcases into the car while she changed.

At Kennedy, I wished her well on her coverage of the Falkland Islands a few years after the invasion.

19

"Thanks, honey," she said. "Feels good, your pulling for me the way you do."

"It's easy. You're a promising writer. Remember?"

"You're not so bad yourself. Your summer project will be super."

"Think so?"

"Know so. Just get it done." She pinched my cheeks like a mother trying to shape a son. "I want to see a rough draft when I get back."

The loudspeaker blared the final call for boarding. Without another word, Mindy's eyes looked deep into mine as if she were trying to draw courage from them. Then she softened, wrapped her arms around my neck, gave me a long wet kiss, and headed for the plane. I watched that head with the bouncy feather cut, that lovely slender form in a chic suit, those lovely calves and small feet.

I watched her every move as she passed the gate attendant and headed down the gangway. Once she stopped, turned, gave me a long last look, and waved.

I waved, too, but weakly. Most of my energy had gone into controlling an urge to call out to her. Tell her to come back. Ask her to sit down with me and figure out how both of us could be together for the summer. But that would be weakness, and it was resisting such Siren calls that had made us precious to each other.

As I drove away from Kennedy, I felt a lump in my throat as big as a golf ball. But by the time I crossed the Whitestone Bridge, all my mental forces were gearing up for the next day's writing session.

As I pulled into my driveway, the screen door of the next house opened, and out popped Luke Bell, the giant teenager who lived there. He wore ragged cut-offs, an orange T-shirt commemorating his attendance at a Dire Straits rock concert, and paint-spattered running shoes so old some of his toes were showing. By the time the screen door had slammed, he was halfway to the car.

"Hey, Barnaby," he said. "How are ya? Did ya miss the place? How was the assignment? Are ya glad to be back?" The husky blond high schooler placed both hands on the open window of the car door and peered in at me. My gaze focused first on those big hands. Then I studied Luke's face with its steel-blue eyes before I spoke. A dimple was punched into each cheek and a wide—very wide—grin stretched across, much closer to one ear.

"Well hello there, Mr. Charmball. Let's see. To answer your questions: I'm fine. I missed the place. The assignment went well. I'm glad to be back." I continued to look into his face and waited. The longer I waited, the wider he stretched the grin.

"Any more questions?" I prompted.

Luke snickered, then faked toughness. "No more questions, Barnaby. Just pay me what you owe me."

"See there?" I replied. "When you wait long enough, you get the bottom line."

"I'm taking Maggie to a concert. Wanta get tickets to Crosby, Stills, and Nash. At Jones Beach. Long Island. Need money."

Sensing somebody behind him, I looked at the ground between Luke's feet-apart stance and spied a small pair of well-shaped legs ending in red sneakers.

"Don't tell me, Luke. You're still going with that little troublemaker Maggie Hannigan— the one who's been hanging around you since junior high, the one who always wears *red shoes?* If I've warned you once, I've warned you 209 times to stay away from her."

Just then Maggie poked her blond bob around Luke. Her perky little face was twisted into a superserious frown, but the tightly pressed-together lips couldn't hide her grin.

"Well, hello, Maggie," I said. "I didn't see you standing there. I suppose you're this big guy's back-up. If I don't pay him, he'll sic you on me."

"You got it, Barnaby," she said.

"Okay," I said, getting out of the car. "Let's check the place out."

The couple followed silently while I circled the yard, front and back, looking closely at the well-kept lawn, the hedges, the carefully nurtured morning glories climbing the trunk of the oak tree in front of the house, and the strip of freshly exploded orange tigerlilies that separated my front lawn from Soundview Avenue.

Actually, I didn't have to check. The kid was good at taking care of my place, and had been for the past six years. Even the mail had been carefully separated into four cardboard boxes —first class, magazines, newsletters, junk mail—all placed side by side on the floor of my office.

And he had closed a hole in the hedge between my property and the train tracks by putting down two posts with wire mesh between them. He knew how much I feared a youngster might run through the hedge and slide down the embankment onto the four tracks. The electric commuter trains on the outside tracks picked up speed rapidly and made little noise. The two inner tracks were worse. When I was nine, I had lost a close friend down there. The high-speed AMTRAK on the inside track moved so fast it had arrived before the sound of its engines and caught Jimmy unaware. Only a loud blast of the whistle could have pierced the air and alerted him, but the engineer hadn't seen him in time.

I paid Luke the going rate and enough extra to put wide grins on both their faces.

"Tell you what," I suggested. "Have Crosby, Stills, and Whatever play my favorite song."

"Uh . . . Well, what's the name of it?" Luke asked.

" 'Sentimental Journey.' "

They looked at each other, grabbed their throats, and faked retches. Maggie, recovering first, planted a kiss on my cheek, and Luke punched me lightly on the arm. Then they were off and running, hand in hand, jabbering joyously, heading for her house a couple of blocks away.

The bank clock at the diagonal corner of the square declared 7:31 P.M., time to gear up for my big project. I went to my office and tackled the mail. Junk mail had gone directly into the waste basket, unopened. Crucial correspondence received instant replies on the bottoms and backs of the letters. Those that could wait were flipped into a large box and shoved into a closet for the summer.

I positioned a file box full of interview notes on the left side of the word processor and took two tattered, heavily marked books from the shelf—Oates' *Let the Trumpet Sound: The Life of Martin Luther King* and Naisbitt's best seller, *Megatrends*. These I placed on the other side of the keyboard. I put Aussie journalist John Hawke's envelope beside the books, figuring I'd read his newsclips when I had a few minutes' down time.

After loading the printer with a fresh stack of continuous-feed paper, I had paused, looking reverently at the setup. Then I went to bed.

☆   ☆   ☆

I snapped out of my reminiscing when I suddenly saw the bank sign flashing 2:02 P.M. I slammed my fist on the desk, rolled off my chair, dropped to the floor, and did thirty push-ups.

When I sat down again, my heart was pumping robust pulses of blood through my body. Such frantic bursts usually help get the creative juices flowing.

Not this time. At 4:00 the screen was still blank—a whole day wasted.

Oh, well, I thought, every writer has such bummer days. I splashed water in my face, changed shirts, and headed across to Vittorio's Diner.

"Welcome home, friend," came a voice as I

passed the postoffice. Postmaster Abe Goodkin, a feisty little man with a balding head, was standing in the doorway.

"I've missed hearing about your current scheme for uncorrupting governments, drying every eye, and wiping hate off the face of the earth." Abe's happy smile split his kind, red-cheeked face. "Too many grim realists around here."

"Yeah," I said, "and you're the grimmest of them all."

"That's okay, I still need a description of your latest organizing principle so I don't lose my sense of humor." When he chuckled, the lids almost closed over his eyes—eyes that at a very early age had seen hell.

And yet, Abe had an uncanny way of seeing something funny in every tough situation that came along. It made you want to believe that God himself must possess a sense of humor like Abe's, a humor that kept Him from giving up on the people of Planet Earth.

"I've missed you, Abe. Mindy told me there was an epidemic of flu while I was gone. Hope it didn't get you."

"Barnaby, how could I get the flu? I survived Auschwitz. Remember?"

"There you go again. I wish you could help me write like you talk."

"Make me an offer!" He laughed and turned to go back to work.

I stepped into the news and magazine store and found the O'Rourke twins standing side by side behind the counter. Both pudgy redheads had freckled faces that almost matched their hair.

"Welcome home, Barnaby," Kevin said softly, smiling. Although always friendly, both were unusually shy for twenty-five-year-old men—so shy I never felt close to them. Nevertheless, I kept trying.

"Thanks, Kevin," I said, my voice matching his. "Good to be back. How's the bicycle riding?"

"Sean and I just bought a couple of Puch Ultimas."

"Good bikes?"

"Top of the line."

"You two are something else. As long as I can remember, you've loved bicycles like other men love their wives. No wonder you're still single."

Both men blushed, went silent.

"No doubt I'll see the two of you riding around town," I said, trying to salvage the conversation. "By the way, do you have any back copies of the *New York Times*?"

Sean nodded sheepishly.

"I'll pick them up on my way home," I said, and walked on to the diner.

Pete Vittorio saw me enter and dropped his spatula, the smile wide under his black handlebar mustache as he came at me. His two hands squeezed mine like a vise.

"Hey, Maureen," he called toward the back room. "Toast a bagel and put chicken salad on it."

"Don't tell me. Barnaby Shane's back!"

An Irish face with black hair cut like Prince Valiant's peered around the corner. "Come to mother, babee." Her white apron failed to hide the lithe form that whipped around the counter. She pulled me close.

"Tell me," Maureen demanded. "How did this barrel-chested Italian ever take me away from you?"

"He looks like Burt Reynolds," I explained. "His muscles are bigger. He's always been kind to you. He decides things quickly while I'm still standing around pondering. But the thing that really did it was that curly black hair on his chest."

"Right." Pete pulled on the open collar of his shirt. "Gets 'em every time."

In spite of our laughter, Maureen sensed something wrong. With her arms still around my neck, she leaned back and looked into my

28

eyes. Her face became mothering, something I enjoyed even though we were the same age.

"You're troubled," she said.

"I didn't know it showed," I replied.

"You had a fight with Mindy?" Pete said.

"Naw," I answered. "Just tired."

"We can fix that," Maureen said.

A few minutes later my favorite bagel sandwich and a cup of coffee were before me. My spirits rose with the taste of oregano-seasoned chunks of chicken as big as gaming dice, squeezed between a warm, toasted bagel made by my two friends from childhood.

I opened up about current happenings in Australia and how I had become so attracted to the honesty and unpretentiousness of certain people in Tasmania and the state of Victoria. I told them Aussies consider it rude to honk automobile horns—except to stop an accident or save a life—that tipping for service has no place in their lives and that they befriended me, greeting me with warm phrases like "Good dye, mite" and "Good on ya."

Pete and Maureen filled me in on the latest happenings in town. Rocco Delmonico had won ten thousand dollars in last week's lottery. Somebody named Rupert Jones had jumped off the station platform in front of the Montreal Express. Auto thefts in the railroad station parking lot on the other side of the tracks had risen to an average of five per week.

Maureen described how little Grover Rassmussen had come off the train from New York a week ago and called his wife, Odette, from the diner's pay phone. He told her he was working late and she'd have to go to the school board meeting without him. Then later, she happened to be walking past the diner.

"When Grover looked up from his meal and saw Odette standing over him hissing like a cobra, he jumped up. I thought he was going to turn around and run through the wall."

"I can't figure it out," Pete said. "Why she goes to school board meetings is a puzzle. The Rassmussens have no children."

"It happens in Soundview," I commented.

Soundview Township's ten-thousand population fell into three categories—winners, winner trainees, and immigrants. The winners were those who had become successes in New York City. The winner trainees were those under pressure to make it in the Big Apple or leave. But the sturdy keel was composed of descendants of Irish and Italian immigrants who built the railroad between New York and Boston in the late 1800s and then had the good sense to settle down on Throttle Hill, the highest ground between the two bustling cities. The three of us and Mindy

Guthrie were members of the latter group and proud of it. Kevin and Sean O'Rourke had immigrant ancestors, too, but they were never as vocal about their roots as we were.

Maureen was preparing to serve up another juicy happening when she suddenly spied something out the front window.

"There they go again," she said.

Turning to look, I saw the two teenagers from Block Five. They leaned forward in their vehicles, eyes front, jaws set as if they were police officers on an emergency call.

"Who are they?" I asked.

"They showed up in town a couple of weeks ago," Pete said. "Saw them once in the supermarket with a black couple—a tall slender woman and the new Soundview police officer. He's at least six-six—looks like a tight end for the New York Giants."

"And these two wheel around town like that?" I said.

"You kidding?" Pete said. "They've been criss-crossing from one end to the other like crazy."

"They take risks, too," Maureen added. "On blocks with curbs, they wheel along the street, passing parked cars on the outside."

"Don't they ever stop in?" I said.

"Nope," Pete said. "And I even installed that ramp three years ago. First time I saw them, I thought I'd get some more customers. So far, no deal."

"Don't they talk to anybody?" I asked.

"They never stop long enough," Maureen said.

"I've seen folks from another country act like that at first," Pete said. "They're afraid they won't be accepted."

"Maybe so," Maureen commented. "But it's going to be hard ignoring those two!"

When I left the diner, I headed back down Front Street, picked up the *Times* back issues at the O'Rourkes', and crossed Soundview Avenue. Then instead of going home, I turned left and walked on to Block Five.

AS I APPROACHED THE HOUSE I SAW THE PAIR ON THE PORCH.

3

The woman Pete had mentioned was there, too, sitting on a porch swing, knitting.

"Hello," I said as I tried to decide whether to walk up the steps or the ramp, then took the ramp.

"I'm Barnaby Shane, and . . . " I stopped abruptly when both teenagers lurched forward until they were hunchbacked, their faces blank, looking past me as if I weren't there.

"I'm Laura Roberts," the woman said, her voice a warm, confident-sounding contralto. She brought her tall, angular frame to its full height, moved toward the young people, and placed a cinnamon-tinted hand on each one's shoulder.

"This is Joe Gamble," she said, nodding toward the young man.

"Pleased to meet you, Joe." I held out a hand.

Joe remained frozen.

"And this is Jessica Packard."

"Happy to meet you, Jessica." I extended my hand again.

The young woman shunned me just as Joe had.

"Hey, you two. Aren't you going to answer Mr. Shane?"

Both remained hunched over, eyes fixed as if they were looking at something across the street.

"Please excuse my two friends," Mrs. Roberts said with an arresting smile and a wink, and without the slightest hint of embarrassment. "They're really nice. But like all teenagers these days, they have minds of their own, and sometimes they're hard to figure out."

"I know what the trouble is." I told her about the accident and my big mouth. The pair remained detached, as if they didn't hear a word.

After my confession, I waited for a tough sermon from Mrs. Roberts. It never came. Instead, she asked if I were all right.

"I'm fine," I said. "Just a little sore here and there."

34

Then, hands on hips, she turned to Joe and Jessie.

"You two," she said to the young people, with a combination smile and frown. "You never said anything about this."

"Sometimes that's an admirable way to be. They . . . " I stopped. It struck me that I was talking past them. "I mean, Joe and Jessica, that a lot of people speak before they think . . . like me."

Joe suddenly looked at me, rolled his eyes in disgust, went back into his inner fortress, and slammed the door. I could tell he wasn't about to let me wound him a second time.

Mrs. Roberts spoke again, a soft wooing note in her voice. "Sam and I told you moving here wasn't going to be a piece of cake. Remember?"

"Look," I said to them, trying to make my voice even softer than Mrs. Robert's. "When I said that, I didn't think it would get through."

Jessie turned to me and opened her mouth. A soft groan came from deep within her throat as her lips tried unsuccessfully to close around sounds and shape them into words. Her arm thrust forward, then dropped to a masonite board on her lap. It was over a foot wide and about a foot and a half long. Printed on the board were the alphabet, basic numbers, and a series of often-used phrases. Looking closely,

I saw her index finger touch a phrase: "I can hear perfectly." She looked me straight in the eye.

At a loss for words, I just stood there. Then Joe's wheelchair swung sideways and touched me softly on the leg. Unlike Jessie, he made no soft noise, but his arm also went down on his board. His index finger pointed to another phrase: "Please repeat as I talk (This is how I talk—by spelling words)." He looked at me and waited.

I nodded.

Then he touched the phrase, "I can hear perfectly."

As soon as I said, "Yes, I see," his hand moved slowly over the board. I repeated the letters he touched: "D . . . o . . . y . . . o . . . u . . . ?"

"Do you? Do I what?" I repeated it again. Then his double meaning finally dawned on me. There was nothing for me to do but slowly nod.

Then Jessie's chair banged me and her hand went into motion again.

"Some ABs think we are vegetables," she spelled. Without disturbing the communication between me and the teenagers, Mrs. Roberts quietly explained that AB is their slang for able-bodied people.

Jessie's hands moved again. "We have feelings. Just like ABs."

Then Joe's index finger began pointing: "We don't even consider ourselves handicapped. We just have a different life-style."

"Why can't ABs see that?" Jessie pointed, then looked at me as if she were ready for a fistfight.

They watched me and waited.

"Look. I'm sorry, I'm really sorry for what I said."

Jessie's glare softened, she turned to Joe, and I saw from the tender looks they gave each other that a visual conversation was going on.

Then Joe turned to me and, with all the control he could muster, he slowly spelled, "We're sorry we got in your way."

"No harm done," I said, patting him lightly on the hand.

Backs straightened and hunchbacks disappeared. Arms moved in wild patterns until their inside hands rested affectionately on each other's shoulders. Then slowly their outside hands came together and stretched toward me.

I closed mine around them.

THE NEXT MORNING, I WAS OFF THE BED

4

and out of the house a few seconds after 6:00.

"Wait up, Barnaby. I'll run with you." It was the blond hulk from next door, sprinting to my side.

"Promise to go at my pace?"

"Promise," Luke said.

We took off for the beach.

Joe and Jessie saw us coming and whirred down the ramp.

"Watch out, Luke," I said, laughing, as soon as were within earshot. "Go for the curb." We ran an arc around them, and the young couple's laughter could be heard a block away. Returning to the sidewalk, I called to them that we'd stop in on our way back.

"You know those guys already?" Luke asked.

"You might say I've run into them before."

But when we returned, they were gone.

"They're on a stake-out," Mrs. Roberts said through the screen door. "Sam and I are having a morning cup. Join us."

I felt a momentary surge of resentment because Joe and Jessica hadn't waited. But they did indeed have minds of their own. Just because I had managed what I thought was a gracious reaching out to them, they weren't about to orbit their lives around mine.

When we entered the kitchen, Mr. Roberts —his huge frame filling out a well-pressed patrolman's uniform—stood up and held out an oversized hand. When he closed it around mine, I expected a knuckle crusher, but it had a gentleness that could be trusted with baby birds. His eyes were wide and receptive, even when he laughed. But the thing that captured my attention was his long, expressive mouth. We all introduced ourselves, exchanging first names.

"Good to meet you," Sam said, his voice a smooth, comforting bass. "Barnaby, I heard about the subtle way the Jays introduced themselves yesterday. The Jays—that's what we call them, since both their first names start with J. You must be an all-right guy if you can get teenagers that close to you." His mouth widened into an arresting smile. "Just don't try to con me into believing you know what makes them tick." He winked at Luke, and we all laughed.

Laura came in with a hot mug for me, then poured Luke a large glass of milk and told him to help himself to doughnuts. The aroma that reached my nose signaled a coffee richer than the average. When I experienced its smooth satin taste, I had to tell her it was light years better than the brewed-from-tarpaper beverage I experienced on the road.

"Why, thank you," Laura said. "When I went to Columbia, I worked nights at the Waldorf Astoria. Learned their tricks."

"I can see that," I said. "But tell me, what's this about Joe and Jessie going on . . . a stake-out?"

"My husband has this terrible habit of discussing police work at the kitchen table." Laura lovingly tapped Sam's arm, her brown eyes looking warmly into his.

Sam turned to me with a look of pained innocence. "I only said that twenty cars had been stolen in the station parking lot this past month."

"Yeah," Laura said, "and three seconds later, the Jays announced via their communication boards that they would be spending the day on the hill that overlooks the lot."

Sam shook his head and again his mouth stretched into a wide grin. "That's the Jays for you. They're going to prove to this town that they have something to give, if it kills them."

"If they stay on the hill, someone named Odette Rassmussen will be happy," Laura said.

"What's this?" I asked.

"Some woman in town," Laura explained. "She gave us a call two days ago. Said she was a concerned citizen with a deep commitment for the safety and the quality of the community. She felt it was her duty to inform us that if our two young people kept whizzing around on their machines, sooner or later they would hit some old woman and break her legs."

Luke and I exchanged glances; then I asked Laura how she had responded.

"I thanked her for telling us."

"That's all?"

"That's all."

"Don't let her get away with that," I said.

"You think that's rough," Sam said. "Let me tell you about the lady from Welcome Wagon."

"Sam. Stop." Laura said.

Sam didn't. "And you should have seen the look on the principal's face when we told him Joe and Jessie would be enrolling in high school this fall. Now that will be one tough, uphill . . . "

"Saaam. Shut up!" Laura said.

Sam laughed and paused for a sip of coffee. "You know, fellows, life isn't fair." He took another sip. "But sometimes you can manipulate it." Then his mouth formed a wide crescent again.

I looked straight into Sam's eyes, trying to see if he were on the level. I saw steadiness and a kindly sparkle . . . and I nodded, letting him know I "heard him perfectly."

"Sam began his world-changing manipulations at a rather early age," Laura began.

"How'd he do that?" I asked.

"Well, it goes back to 1955." Laura related that nine-year-old Sam had left New York City to spend Christmas vacation with his aunt in Montgomery, Alabama. His aunt lived next door to Rosa Parks, the black woman who, in that Christmas season, was arrested on a city bus because she refused to give up her seat to a white man. Sam had come to know and love Mrs. Parks, and he couldn't stand to see her humiliated. So he joined with the neighborhood kids and took special training in nonviolent political action from a young minister named Martin Luther King, Jr. Then they moved through the black community with leaflets calling for the Montgomery bus boycott.

"You're kidding," Luke said. "I read about Rosa Parks in school. She triggered a whole new era of social justice in our country."

"I suppose she did," Sam said. "And ever since, justice—in one form or another—has been my bag."

Luke asked about the stolen cars.

"So far it proves that crime can pay," Sam said. "Some individuals—well-organized individuals—are making a lot of money."

"Really?" Luke said.

"Almost twenty thousand cars were stolen in Connecticut last year. New York state went over a hundred thousand. Only half are recovered, and only 15 percent lead to arrests. And let's not talk about convictions."

"Wow," Luke said.

Seeing he had our attention, Sam explained. A thief can use a "Morgan knocker"—a foot-long device that screws into the key slot on a car door—and jerk the lock cylinder out as if it were a radish. He does the same to the ignition lock. Then he jams a screwdriver into the switch, turns it, and within thirty-two seconds from the time he first touched the car, he's driving away.

Sam felt there must be an organization in New York so big it puts out a daily list of models and colors in demand by body shops and overseas buyers. Scouts spot the precise models and call headquarters, which dispatches men to steal them. The three-hundred-fifty-car parking lot on Throttle Hill had the

43

record for the most thefts, because there it's so easy to get off a train, into a car, and onto I-95.

According to Sam's theory, some cars are driven right onto ships ready to embark for ports all over the world. Others go to area "chop shops." Within twenty-four hours, a car is broken down into parts for body-repair shops, providing a certain "nose"—bumper, grill, hood, and front fenders—or "rear clip" —the body from the middle door post to the rear bumper. Other parts are stocked and listed as available via legitimate commercial electronic networks used by parts dealers and auto repair shops.The frames, chassis, and lock cylinders are disposed of rapidly since they contain identification numbers.

And, although it's extremely hard to prove, some disappear in "double-dip" insurance fraud. The owner receives a cash sum from a thief and arranges for the "theft" of his car. He can even make it easy for the crook. Later, the owner collects full value from his insurance company.

A few adolescents see keys dangling in ignition switches and, yielding to a devilish urge, drive off just for the heck of it. These vehicles, however, are usually found elsewhere in the county, sometimes wrecked.

Sam held Luke and me spellbound with his

information. Then I asked if the Jays knew all this.

"They know more, thanks to Officer Big Mouth," Laura said with a note of humor. "He talks to them as if they were in the police academy."

"Well, Joe has a detective mind, and Jessie is the most supportive partner he could have."

Laura sighed. "Your head is in the clouds, Sam. You're expecting too much."

"It's okay to give them a few dreams, honey."

"A few dreams, maybe. But must you give them Cinerama? You could be pumping them up for a terrible fall."

"Well, Laura, you're the special ed teacher. Should I back off?"

"Well . . . not yet."

Sam looked at his watch, got up, and leaned over to give Laura a kiss. "Stay and enjoy," he said to Luke and me.

Laura poured refills for both of us. Then I asked about Joe and Jessie.

She described the Jays as two sharp-witted teenagers who happen to have severe cases of cerebral palsy. According to her, they are excellent receivers of sights and sounds, maybe better than most. But when they try to respond to the surrounding world, their muscles go berserk. Arms flail and heads bob.

Sometimes when they become too emotional, try too hard to communicate, their muscles go into painful cramps. Drooling results because their swallowing muscles fail to function efficiently.

And so they exert tremendous thought and energy in controlling their muscles even as well as they do. They also expend great amounts of energy in correcting posture deformities caused by years of lying on mats without physical therapy while painful muscle spasms twisted them out of shape. According to Laura, it takes at least twenty times more energy for the Jays to get up, wash, and dress than for the average person—which accounts for their being so beautifully slim.

Until recently, many professionals assumed that people with cerebral palsy were retarded. Of course, some are—just as some able-bodied persons are. But this single blanket misconception accounted for hundreds of people with these muscle problems being forced to live on wards in large, overcrowded institutions with common denominator rules, like soldiers in training. Quite often those settings denied them the thing they needed most: to be seen as individuals; to be relaxed with, as individuals; and to be slowly and patiently listened to, as individual human beings.

Laura got to know the Jays three years ago,

when she received her master's degree and took a teaching position at High Ridge Developmental Center, an institution thirty miles west of town. Joe and Jessie were students in her class, and she noticed from the first day how much the two had taken to each other. They insisted on sitting together. They helped each other study. When one became ill and couldn't attend, the other seemed ill, too.

Joe lived on a ward with thirty men who had severe disabilities. On the other side of a vast central green, Jessie lived on a similar ward with the same number of women. Their chances of being together resembled a lottery, since the scheduling of programs came from an impersonal central office. Staff members constantly came and went in shifts, and they were so busy maintaining the group regimen, they had little time to slow down and listen to individual preferences—especially from those who had such a hard time communicating.

Laura saw that the regimental existence at High Ridge threatened to frustrate and snuff out what was flowering between the two. She began sharing her concerns with Sam, night after night in bed . . . until at midnight on April 2, he told her to get up and make a pot of her famous coffee. All night long they threw issues into the discussion hopper—his graduation in June from City College of New York with a degree in criminal justice, his acceptance as a police officer in Soundview, the floor space in the Soundview house they planned to rent, the financial loss if Laura quit her job, the smaller government payment for becoming foster parents. At 4:30 A.M. they decided to go for it.

The Roberts invited the Jays to Soundview for a series of "friendly weekend visits."

Thoughtful Joe corrected that right off the bat. "You really mean trial visits," he spelled.

Slowly but surely during the visits, the problems connected with mealtimes, bathing, toileting, dressing, and grooming were ironed out.

On one trial visit, however, Jessie was so overwhelmed by the pressure to succeed that she went into cramps every time she tried a new task. When Joe couldn't stand seeing her suffer anymore, he maneuvered his chair directly in front of her and looked deep into her eyes. Then his face went blank, his good posture disappeared as he slumped forward in his chair. Jessie did, too. They remained like question marks for better than an hour—until Sam the clown caught them off-guard and got them laughing.

Sam and Laura laid out their plans before two interprofessional teams—each consisting of an educator, a psychologist, a physician, a social worker, physical and speech therapists, and three shifts of ward leaders—each having the power to approve or disapprove any program plan for Joe or Jessie. After two sessions with Jessie's team and four with Joe's, Laura and Sam received not only approval, but offers from staff members to travel to Soundview for consultation when their specific expertise was needed.

Then came the matter of parent and guardian approval. Since Jessie had been admitted to High Ridge at age eight, shortly after her mother and father had been killed in a truck-car accident, extra paperwork had to be initiated with the state and a named guardian Jessie had never met. But by then, High Ridge social workers had become advocates for the placement, and the paperwork was completed in record time.

Joe's parents, Morley and Nan Gamble, lived in Colorado, where Mr. Gamble operated heavy equipment for a county department of roads. The Gambles had moved there from Connecticut when Joe was five. The Roberts' first call to them came as a shock. It was the first contact they had had since their talk with a social worker at the time of Joe's admission at age two. That social worker, possessing the "wisdom" of another age, had told them their two-year-old was "a hopelessly and profoundly retarded vegetable." He would never know them. Although the worker neither encouraged nor discouraged visiting, he advised them to "make a fresh life without Joseph." He had comforted the Gambles with a phrase now used more by insurance agents than helping professionals: "He's in good hands now." The chief social worker's office had assigned a professional to keep in touch with the Gambles. But with the early worker's words still ringing in their ears, they had moved west, not thinking to send a change of address to High Ridge. They could have been traced, of course, but professionals were forever coming and going, and the average caseload for social workers was over two hundred.

Now, according to Laura, the Gambles telephone every weekend and let go with a barrage of questions. What's Joe been doing this week? What was the name of that book you said he read? He's really sharp, huh? How's that wheelchair with the motor on it? Would he like our picture? If we save up for plane tickets, do you think he would like to see us? Joe (with Laura or Sam voicing his answers) had responded with the graciousness of a saint. A visit is planned in the fall when Mr. Gamble gets his vacation.

Other bureaucratic technicalities almost

scuttled the prospect in early May—until High Ridge staff members helped the Roberts get to a Big Bureaucrat with the power to kick behinds. Then the foster care plan was quickly authorized and the deal was sweetened with extra money for a special whirlpool tub and two motorized wheelchairs.

I could tell from the way Luke was listening he could have stayed with Laura all day, but I had to get to work. Laura told us to come back.

"C'mon, Barnaby," Luke said. "Let's run the last five blocks."

"After all we ate and drank?"

"Sure."

"Joe and Jessie are something else," he said after we had run a block.

"Sure are."

"And Sam and Laura. They're really nice."

"They're nice. But you're not."

"Why?"

"If you keep going so fast, you're going to kill me."

After running over the I-95 overpass, we angled across the street to see if the Jays were still on their stake-out. We found them fifteen yards from the sidewalk in a circle of bushes overlooking the railroad station parking lot.

Although they had seen Luke earlier, I made a formal introduction. Fingers moved over communication boards rapidly, and I could see it was all meant for Luke. He spelled out their words and phrases and responded with his own.

I stood there thinking how bewildering it is when teenagers talk to one another and make others feel as if they weren't even there. I told the three I had to leave . . . had lots of work to do . . . I was going . . . good-bye. The three managed slight farewell nods, then put their heads together and went at it again.

MY DAY WENT WELL.

5

I organized principles and supporting facts into the beginning of an outline and glanced periodically at the three teenagers. From my window, it was easy to look down into the bushes on the other side of the railroad overpass.

Their lookout spot was perfect; it resembled duck blinds used by hunters. The watchers couldn't be seen from the sidewalks, streets, overpasses, or commuter platforms. And yet they could peer through the bushes in all directions and down into the parking lot, an area the size of a football field which filled the hollow between the highway and the train tracks. They could observe the three hundred-plus cars left for the day by commuters, and any car moving on the driveway to Soundview Avenue (the only access road) passed within twenty feet of them.

Luke stayed with his friends for better than an hour. They talked. They peered between the bushes. And every time a car came or went, Joe worked a gadget that was sitting on his communication board while the other two watched.

After Luke left, Joe and Jessie continued to keep a watch in their jungle, like Tarzan and Jane must have peered through foliage, trying to discern good forces from evil ones. Once in a while they paused for long looks at each other. And when nothing was happening, they sat side by side, holding hands.

I thought about what it must have been like to live in those large, institutional wards Laura had described, and how different life must be for the Jays, now that they reside with just two people, in an ordinary house, on an ordinary block.

I thought about the monstrous images that even the name of the institution had created in people's minds. The jibe, "Hey man, you're ready for High Ridge" had been spoken by ordinary citizens as far back as I could remember. Anyone driving through the town of High Ridge couldn't miss the large smokestack, the water tower, and the ten three-story buildings on a hill overlooking the town. When I was a child, the place was called the State Institute for the Feebleminded, and more than two thousand people—more people than were in the town—lived up there. Although everyone knew the place, it was seldom in the news, and anybody who had a relative there usually kept it quiet.

Now, however, the High Ridge population had dwindled to a couple hundred, and many of the buildings were empty. Most of the people had moved quietly into community settings.

In some cases, however, neighbors raised a rumpus about these people with disabilities coming onto their block. From the noise the complainers made, one tended to think they were the majority.

I thought about Odette Rassmussen. She had drawn a bead on the Jays already. She could organize our neighborhood against them.

Two years earlier, Odette and Grover Rassmussen had settled on Soundview Avenue, in a house on the other side of the Bell family. Odette was a small, sinewy woman in her late forties. The everchanging color and style of her hair reflected frequent visits to the beauty parlor. She could have been attractive if she didn't set her jaw and pinch her face together, always looking so deadly serious about everything. Her husband Grover wasn't much bigger. He had a small round face with hundreds of tiny broken blood vessels that gave his cheeks a crimson hue. A single narrow band of graying hair stretched around the back of his head from one ear to the other. He could usually be seen going to and from the commuter station in a gray pin-stripe suit that could have been purchased in a boys' department. Nevertheless, Grover could be an all-right guy when his wife wasn't around.

According to Odette, she and Grover came from the best families in Baltimore. She spoke incessantly in her high-pitched voice about Johns Hopkins this and Johns Hopkins that, her lips forming the words as if she had a plum in her mouth. Grover was a wizard with figures, she said. He had been appointed manager of large investments at Metro City Savings in New York City. He was moving up so fast, she said, the couple would be relocating soon to the more "refined" section of Soundview. In the meantime, Odette had chosen to give herself to the betterment of our street.

That, of course, made me one of her prime targets. On certain days she would take off toward me with rapid, mincing steps like a windup toy. Seeing her on the march, I would casually move to the right or left of her path, but she would correct her course until we were face to face. Then she would lecture me for fronting my place with those "terrible weeds some people call tigerlilies" and for leaving beer cans on my lawn too long after they had been tossed from passing cars.

Throwing parties too big for my small house always got me a blast the next morning. Even so, her lectures motivated me to overfertilize my tigerlilies, hold more parties than I needed to, and leave cans lying around longer than they should have.

I didn't feel as cocky, however, when I thought about Odette's sudden interest in Joe and Jessie.

☆　☆　☆

At 5:09 P.M., the first peak-scheduled commuter from New York City rolled into the station. A river of people flowed out of the train onto the platform as if a dam had broken. Waves of people entered their cars and drove either to Soundview Avenue where they turned right or left, or went straight across to the entrance ramp of I-95. The Jays moved from behind the bushes and headed back up to the sidewalk.

I went outside and stood in the front yard where they could see me. When they did, their arms flew into the air and I went to meet them.

"How'd things go?" I asked.

"Gathering raw evidence," Jessie spelled. She pointed to a small hand-held, battery-powered instrument on Joe's board. It had a keyboard for numbers and alphabet, and it printed messages on a quarter-inch paper tape that came out the side like an old-fashioned tickertape machine. The description and license plate of every car driving in and out during the day had been recorded. They had also recorded the descriptions and movements of certain pedestrians. Joe grasped the instrument and slowly worked it into the knapsack attached to the back of Jessie's chair.

"You missed lunch," I said. "I have frozen TV dinners at my place. What do you say?"

There was no mistaking the moving arms and laughter, so we headed for my place.

My porch stopped us. It was a cement slab eight inches higher than the sidewalk, but with their heavy machines, it could have been a hundred-foot cliff. The pair stared at the step, then at me.

"I'm sorry," I said.

Joe's fingers moved over the board.

"It's okay. We are probably your first friends with a life-style that rules out steps."

"Well, you're gracious about it."

Joe looked into my face and, with perfect control and a cocky smile, nodded agreement.

"Got an idea," I said. "The diner down the street has a ramp. Let's go there."

Their laughter was richer and more free, and I knew they would rather have gone there in the first place.

After my formal introduction, Pete and Maureen welcomed the couple, who spelled their pleased-to-meet-yous. In less than a minute the Vittorios got the hang of the communication boards. I left them and walked to the pay phone at the other end of the diner to call Laura Roberts.

"I'm at Vittorio's Diner with Joe and Jessie," I said. "Is it okay for them to have supper with me?"

"You're in for it now," she said.

"Why? Some problem with how or what they eat?"

"Not at all. They'll tell you how to help them. It's just that once those two get a foothold in that diner!" She laughed. "Just wait and see."

As I returned, four grinning faces stared at me.

"What's going on?" I said.

"Just got the truth," Pete said.

"What truth?" I said.

"The one about how you got creamed by their machines," Pete said. "That's what I call *striking* up a friendship."

More loud laughter from the Jays. For a moment I wondered why they laughed so much, but my wonderment faded as I watched Maureen lean over to get the spelling for two orders of the evening special—pot roast, mashed potatoes and gravy, green beans, milk, and Maureen's wonderful dinner rolls. I really didn't care much for pot roast, but I ordered the same with coffee.

Maureen came forth with heaping plates of food. At Jessie's request, I cut their meat, buttered their rolls, and periodically held their milk glasses steady until they could grip them. When they began to eat, my facial muscles stretched and moved in an unconscious attempt to help guide their spoons from plate to mouth. But after seeing that their circuitous approaches always ended successfully, I relaxed and enjoyed the lively mealtime communion. Pete and Maureen added to it by hovering over us every now and then. People at other tables paid little attention except when we laughed a lot. Then I noticed others smiling.

Halfway through our meal, Odette walked in with Grover and, in her voice that carries so well, told him she had been too busy to fix supper. He would "just have to eat at the diner and like it." One could never tell what

Grover liked or didn't like when he was with his wife.

"Hi, Grover. Hello, Odette," I said.

"Hi, Barnaby," Grover said blandly. He turned to Joe and Jessica. "Hello, how are you?" The Jays nodded.

Odette surveyed us for a moment like an authoritarian parent preparing to check for clean ears.

"Why, hello, Mr. Shane. I see you have become acquainted with our new neighbors. Did they have any trouble getting those machines into the diner?"

"No problem, Odette." My face burned because she talked *about* Joe and Jessica when she should have addressed them directly. I answered quickly. It was the only way to keep her off guard.

"Well, that's nice," she said, smiling like a barracuda. "As you can see, Mr. Rassmussen and I will be having supper at this . . . uh . . . diner, too."

"Good for you, Odette."

She and Grover took a table at the far end of the diner, and for the rest of the meal we were under her watchful eye.

The Jays ate everything on their plates, making Maureen so happy she rewarded them with large pieces of pineapple upside-down cake and vanilla ice cream.

I watched with amazement as Joe and Jessie packed the food away, until I recalled that Laura had said they used twenty times as much energy as the average person.

"Want some more?" Pete asked when they had finished.

Joe leaned back, rolled his eyes and smiled, and Jessie worked her arm until she could pat her stomach.

"Look, you two," Maureen said. "Pete and I were talking. Tomorrow is Independence Day; we're closing the diner at 5:30. Gonna have a picnic on Lookout Ledge; we'll be in the best spot for the fireworks in the evening. Go with us. And Mr. and Mrs. Roberts, too?"

"And," Pete added, "if old nose-to-the-grindstone Barnaby will stop trying to save the world for a while, he can come, too."

The Jays paused, looked at each other. Then Jessie straightened her back, held her head high and carefully positioned her board.

With the aplomb of a princess, she spelled, "We would be delighted to accept your invitation, Mr. and Mrs. Vittorio." Prince Joseph, head held just as high, nodded agreement.

Back to the pay phone I went and dialed Laura. Odette, sitting nearby, was all ears. The Roberts agreed to go, but Sam would have to leave during the fireworks display to go on duty.

When the three of us left the diner, Joe and Jessie whirred down Front Street while I tried to keep up, taking the longest steps I could without breaking into a run. At Soundview Avenue, I offered to see them home, but they insisted on going alone.

JULY 4, A LOVELY MORNING.

6

The air was cool and dry; there wasn't a cloud in the sky. I took off for Lookout Ledge with an extra spring in my step.

"Hey Barnaby." It was Luke.

I stopped, arching my back as if I'd been shot.

Luke pulled alongside. "Okay, let's go."

"Wait!"

"What for?"

"Remember yesterday? You promised to keep to my pace."

"Aw, Barnaby. Don't worry. I'll try to keep it down."

Approaching Block Five, we expected to see the Jays on their front porch, but instead we found them waiting for us on the ledge. They were wearing jeans and bright red polo shirts. When we approached, they went into their usual paroxysms of delight.

All hands reached out to Luke and, as teenagers often do, they treated one another as if they were royalty. I was left standing around like a dumb peasant, but I tolerated their behavior philosophically, since I understood the underlying reasons for it—or so I thought.

"Welcome to breakfast," Jessie spelled. Joe dipped into Jessie's knapsack and pulled out an aluminum foil package with four thick ham and egg sandwiches made with homemade bread, still hot. Then came a thermos of milk, a thermos of Laura's special coffee, a cup, and three glasses. I wasn't sure why they had planned for Luke. Did they know he'd be with me, or were they merely hoping he would?

The Jays slid out of their wheelchairs onto the grass, leaving room for a communication board to function as a table in the middle. Luke and I completed the circle.

When breakfast was over, Luke and the Jays, using the remaining board, went at it again, talking back and forth. Later, Luke sensed this elderly serf's watchful but silent presence.

"Know what we learned yesterday, Barnaby?" he said. "All three of us are sixteen. We all have birthdays in October. And we'll all be seniors at Soundview High—that is, if we can get Dr. Sparks, the principal, to change his mind."

"Nice," I said.

"Do something for us, Barnaby," Joe spelled.

"What?"

"Get Luke and Maggie invited to Vittorio's picnic?"

I took a slow sip of coffee. "Afraid not."

"Why?" Jessie spelled.

"Because Maggie will wear red shoes."

Since my answer didn't compute with the Jays, they looked at each other for a time, then their quizzical glances focused on me and saw the smile behind my cup.

Then Joe, with Dick Tracy seriousness, announced that he and Jessie were late for their early morning duty. He suggested that Luke and I finish our run.

"You know, Barnaby," Luke said as we headed home, "Those are neat kids. . . . They're sharp. . . . Can't wait for Maggie to meet them. . . . Nice kids."

With Luke streaking off and me trying to keep up, all I could squeeze out between puffs was, "Right. . . . Yep. . . . Uh-huh. . . . Yeah, Luke."

Finally, I'd had it. As we neared the first overpass, I opened up and sprinted for the house.

He beat me by thirty yards. I barely made my front lawn and went down spread-eagled on my back, taking each breath as if it were my last.

"Barnaby. We gotta get you in shape."

"Shut up."

☆   ☆   ☆

All day my hands moved over the keyboard. Phrases appeared rapidly on the screen, and I tinkered with each one until it felt like a good throw to second base—nothing extra, right on target. I was on a roll.

Productive days make me glad I am a "writer" instead of a "talker." Listening intently to an argument and responding on paper is far more satisfying than using my mouth. I do manage to get into my share of heated oral arguments, but I seldom come up with my best answer right off. At 2:00 the next morning, after hashing and rehashing the issue, my answer becomes as focused and sharp as a rifle shot. My opponents, though, don't take kindly to telephoned rebuttals at such an hour.

For me, writing is a wonderful way of thinking—pondering an issue, writing it out again and again until I can say the most about it in the fewest possible words. The process is painfully slow. I agonize over each word, struggling for the best way to put it on a line with others, but I love doing it. And if fate forced me to decide between brain-to-mouth or brain-to-fingers communication, I would gladly give up the mouth first.

My thoughts on networks were shaping up. After going over boxes of interview notes on small organizations that made the world around them a better place, I found some commonalities: Many began as small motley groups—young and old, different racial, economic, and educational backgrounds—people who suddenly discovered an overpowering force (a certain government, industry, or neighborhood) that was bringing unfair suffering to a defenseless people or to their environment. The issue drew them together as if they had been trapped overnight in an elevator stuck between floors. Most became involved without even knowing they were "networking."

Unlike formal organizations, these movements are not fueled primarily by money, but by the strong urge to share crucial information about a painful situation. And through such sharing, small handfuls of people begin to care deeply for one another—even though some meet only on the telephone. If money is spent, most goes for telephone bills, photocopying, and postage. Out of a network's hunger for justice, a power that is much more than the sum of its working members is generated, and it sometimes changes the attitudes of hundreds of citizens.

The best networkers seem to be incurable optimists. Dishonest players are shunned. Embittered ideologues—even brilliant ones—usually don't last long either.

Most successful networks are informal. They hardly ever are organized from the top down. When they are, they usually become formal committees, councils, task forces, or advisory groups. A true network springs from the heart—not from conscription, appointment, or election.

I was ready to apply actual situations to my theories. But the bank's time and temperature sign flashed a large red 5:10. I had to stop, shower, and get to Lookout Ledge.

AT 5:30, SMALL COLLECTIVES OF PEOPLE

in khakis, jeans, cottons, and colors began setting up on Lookout Ledge. Frisbees and softballs whizzed above the crowd. The din of light-hearted chatter was punctuated occasionally by laughing shouts, the shrill cries of children, or the ear-bashing bang of a firecracker.

We staked our claim, spreading a large red and white checked tablecloth on the grassy top and covering it with containers of chicken and eggplant parmigiana, as well as italian sausage and peppers, all giving off steamy oregano-laced aromas. Sharing the space were a large bowl of antipasto, hot breads, peaches in wine, and an ice chest filled with beer and soft drinks.

Abe Goodkin, the postmaster, was with us, as were Luke and Maggie. Pete and Maureen had invited them all at the last minute, and

70

they had even tried to get the O'Rourke twins to come. But Sean wanted to keep the newspaper store open until ten, and Kevin wanted to pedal to various hills to catch views of the fireworks from different angles.

The young people received their servings first, then went farther out onto the ledge, where Luke's portable radio added a hammering beat and incomprehensible lyrics to the ambiance of their meal. Luke had helped by preparing the Jays' plates while Maggie stood and watched.

"When they go off like that, it makes me feel old," I said.

Sam gave me a quizzical smile. "When they play that kind of music? You've got to be kidding. Don't you have any respect for your ears? Besides, I'm on call." He nodded toward the handheld walky-talky on the ground beside him.

"Maureen and I don't care where they go as long as they like our food," Pete said. "Right, babe?"

Maureen, with her mouth full, nodded and swallowed.

"Your problem, Barnaby." She swallowed again. "If Mindy were here, you wouldn't even know there were any younger people around."

"Probably so," I said. "I guess adolescents need to pull off and develop their own subculture—their own music and clothes and language, their own viewpoints. Otherwise they'd never bring anything fresh to the world."

Abe looked up into the sky. "Mindy, wherever you are, come home. Soundview's solver of world problems now thinks the answer can be found in youth." He laughed and patted me on the back. For years, we had served as relentless foils for each other, and we loved it.

"Go ahead and laugh," I said. "It won't be long before they'll be running the country."

"You're right, Mister Philosopher," Sam agreed, chuckling, "but when they do, we ought to run for the hills!"

"Good for you," Abe said to Sam. "I now have an ally. You come to the postoffice, and I'll see you get cutrate postage stamps."

Just then more of the high school set—several girls and boys—came up the path and joined our four. Luke introduced Joe and Jessie to a couple while the rest gathered around Maggie.

The group started back down the path. Then a lanky Don-Quixote-like, dark-haired fellow in a purple muscle shirt turned back and motioned Maggie aside. They talked. Maggie returned to Luke and the Jays while the young man rejoined his retreating gang.

By the time all of us had eaten our fill, Muscle Shirt and his group were back. Again he conversed with Maggie, who then talked to Luke—until he emphatically shook his head. Maggie stood, hands on hips for a moment, then pranced after the group.

"I can't let this happen," I said, starting up.

Sam placed his hand on my arm. Looking at me, he said a lot by saying nothing.

"What about Joe and Jessie?"

"It's their problem."

"But they're handicapped," I said. "They need support."

"When to support and when to leave people alone—these are the toughest decisions we so-called concerned ones will ever make."

I gave a slow nod. The rest watched and listened.

"Also, Barnaby," Sam continued, "if the Jays heard you use the word *handicapped* in connection with them, they'd shoot up their chins and tell you they are human beings with weaknesses and strengths, just like you and me. They'd tell you they just have a different life-style."

"Maybe so. But what just happened must have hurt. . . . Thank goodness their life-style contains humor. They use laughter like you do, Abe."

Abe nodded.

"Have you been wondering why the Jays laugh so much?" Sam asked me.

"I sure have."

"Laughing is one of their most efficient communications. They will laugh quickly as a signal that they approve of something. But when they're really tickled or it seems like the windows of heaven have opened, their laugh becomes richer. It hits you almost like music."

"The phrases they spell are often like lyrics," Laura added. "And their sentences are short and clean, without adjectives and long, lumbering adverbial embellishments. They have to be that way."

"Why?" I said.

"Because ABs move in and out of their life-space so rapidly. They need to be ready for anyone who slows down to listen for a moment. That's why you'll see them waiting, even calculating, how to make contact with others. After they've connected, it's a different ballgame."

"It's a different ballgame if they're sore at you, too."

Sam laughed. "I heard you got the tune-out treatment."

"You might call it 'stop the music' time."

"Right, and that haunts me," Sam said.

"Why?"

74

"One shouldn't ever hold back the good music that's in people. Laura helped me see that when I was taking course after course in criminal justice. She said I needed to learn something more than how to control people and keep them in line. So I took a course in English literature. It bored me until I read one poem—'Elegy Written in a Country Churchyard.' In the middle 1700s, a man named Thomas Gray sat down in a graveyard and wrote about how often the people under those stones had lived and died with their best talents still unrecognized and undeveloped— still inside. There was one stanza that really touched me:

Perhaps in this neglected spot is laid
    Some heart once pregnant with celestial fire;
Hands that the rod of empire might have
    sway'd,
Or wak'd to ectasy the living lyre.

"Gray's poem was working on me when Laura first came home with stories about Joe and Jessie. In them, I saw lots of . . . "

"Inner music."

"Lots."

"You understand them so well."

"Had a good teacher," Sam said, looking at Laura.

"Joe and Jessie are lucky to have both of you," Abe said.

"The Jays are more lucky to have each other."

"Why?" Pete asked.

"Joe and Jessie understand each other's sounds. At other times they just look at each other and you know they are communicating. Sometimes I can almost sense them saying, 'It's you and me, partner. We've got it together. We'll never be this close with an AB.' "

"Why?"

"A lot of the ABs who've come into their lives these past sixteen years made big promises and then faded."

"But *you* care."

"We do. But we're only human. Think about the grand approach Laura and I have made to Joe and Jessica, working them into our family. If something happens to us, the Jays might be worse off than if we'd never met them."

"But life has to be better for them here," Maureen said, "than living on those wards in High Ridge."

"It is if they can *stay* here," Laura said.

"What's this 'if'?" Abe said.

"One of the conditions of our foster care arrangement calls for a full-service education, and the principal across the street has already told us he couldn't enroll them."

"Why?"

"He was vague. Something about their not fitting in. Sam and I have another appointment, but he's preparing to fight us."

"What if he keeps the Jays out?"

"Don't know. There's a special-training center twenty miles away in Upper Bay. But those two stubborns told us it was Soundview High or nothing."

"That's understandable," I said. "By the way, when it comes to grammar and spelling, they're better than most students. With no schooling earlier in life, how did they get so sharp?"

" 'Sesame Street'."

" 'Sesame Street'?"

"It's hard to believe," Laura explained, "but for years, those two were taken from cribs in the morning and laid on mats or placed upright in chairs during the day, with nothing to do except watch TV. 'Sesame Street' came on quite often. And those two smarties soaked up the alphabet, phonetics, spelling, phrasing, counting, calculating. Then I gave them the communication boards, and both Jays really took off."

"Hungry to learn."

"Starved," Laura agreed.

"But if the school keeps them out, you can teach them, Laura."

"Not now. A parent's job is different from a teacher's. Besides, people learn much from their peers and the setting—maybe more than a teacher teaches." She motioned toward Joe and Jessie and Luke. "See there. Sam and I just hope that . . . "

Laura was interrupted by Sam's radio. The dispatcher ordered him to walk a beat that covered Front Street, the commuter platforms, and the parking lot.

Although the lot was usually empty in the evening, today hundreds of people from nearby townships had parked their cars and taken the trains for the city to watch the celebration on the Hudson River.

"It's not fair," Laura said to Sam.

"It's okay. Wait 'til I make Chief."

Sam got up and went over to the Jays, whose hands reached for his. He slapped Luke on the back, then returned to us.

"By the way," he inquired, "are you people baseball fans?"

"You're asking for trouble," Pete said. "I'd die for the Yanks, and Barnaby has this screwy attraction for the Mets. We argue a lot."

"And I go along to keep them from killing each other," Abe said.

That long, beautiful smile appeared on Sam's face again. "I can get four tickets for the Yanks and Orioles tomorrow night."

Pete, Abe, and I looked at one another with devilish grins. Maureen volunteered to cover the diner alone. The train left at 6:15. If we got off at 125th Street and transferred to the Lexington subway, we could make game time easily.

Sam was leaving when Abe called him back.

"Sam, my friend. I think you're wrong about one thing. If something happened to you and Laura and the Jays had to go back, they might not be worse off." He paused. "Sometimes when things get tough, it's good memories that keep us going."

Without a word, Sam took Abe's hand in both of his. Then he left.

☆   ☆   ☆

The fireworks, launched from a series of offshore barges, seemed louder, brighter, and more resplendent with colorful clusters than ever before. After every starburst, a soft crescendo of "ooohhs" went skyward as if offering an awesome, unison prayer to some great god of fire.

I used the periods of brightness to watch Luke and the Jays. They sat on the ground with Luke in the middle. They all seemed as enthralled as we were.

Late in the display, when five separate pink bursts illuminated the sky, Maggie came up the path and quietly sat behind Luke. During the next flash, I saw the Jays' arms flail a welcome. Then came the finale—twenty red, white, and blue simultaneously fired starbursts that ended with several bright white ear-bashing explosions—and Maggie was sitting beside Jessie, who, in all the excitement, reached over and held her tight.

After the display, the teenagers decided to walk home. The rest of us loaded the picnic gear into the Vittorios' car and drove back up Soundview Avenue.

As soon as I reached home, I checked my answering machine. Mindy had promised to call from Stanley and leave a number. There was no call. I sat quietly for a moment, thinking about all the events of the past three days I wanted to describe to her. Better yet, I wished she had been with us. I had just pulled on a clean pair of purple-and-whites and stretched out on my bed when the phone rang. That's got to be Mindy, I said to myself.

It was Laura, and there was panic in her voice.

SAM HAD BEEN SHOT.

8

His duty sergeant had found him in a pool of blood in the railroad parking lot, and he had been rushed to Soundview Hospital, across the alley from the Immigrant's Trust Bank. He was taken directly into surgery, where a team of five doctors began doing everything they could to keep his life from draining away. The sergeant had hurried to Laura with the news and sped her to the hospital in a squad car, the siren screaming.

Since the Jays and their friends hadn't returned before Laura left, I drove to Block Five and arrived just as they reached the ramp. Quickly, I told them what I knew and asked Luke and Maggie to stay with the Jays for a while. As I hurried to my car, deep-throated sounds came from Joe, and a waving hand landed on his communication board.

"Not now, Joe. I have to hurry."

I came off the elevator on the second floor, glanced at the double doors of the surgery on my right, and crossed the hall to the waiting room. Laura rose from a black vinyl couch and I took her in my arms. She maintained her usual poise, but her soulful brown eyes looked like windows trickling rain. I guided her head to my shoulder, held her tight, and said nothing while she shook silently. After a few moments, she spoke.

"He's been in surgery over an hour." She dried her eyes with tissues from a box on the coffee table. "What will I do if he dies?"

"Put that question on a back shelf and answer this one: What will you do while he's fighting to live?"

"Stay right here."

"Good."

Sensing that someone had entered the room, I turned to see a huge man whose blondish-red eyebrows and mustache stood out like copper scouring pads. Laura introduced Sergeant Callahan. It was he who had found Sam and rushed him to the hospital.

Our introduction was cut short by the whirring of motorized wheelchairs. Into the room came Joe and Jessie, followed by Maggie and Luke.

Laura went down on one knee to face the

Jays at eye level, "I should have known you wouldn't stay away."

Joe made a sound and prepared to spell a message, then gave it up and gazed at Laura. There were no tears, just calmness and kindness in his eyes.

"Sergeant Callahan, this is Mr. Joseph Gamble, my foster son," Laura announced. "And this is my foster daughter, Miss Jessica Packard."

Two hands went out to Sergeant Callahan.

Then Joe's hand went to his communication board. "Sergeant," Luke read as Joe spelled, "Can you tell us what happened?"

Callahan looked at Luke, then at Joe, and finally at Laura.

"Tell him," she said, in a tone that gave Joe the authority he needed.

"Well, sir," Callahan began, "the radio dispatcher reported that someone was triggering their transmitter on and off. Then it stayed on, and the mike apparently was rubbing against clothes. It made a loud grating noise in our speaker. Then came shots. Since Sam was alone, I thought of him first and headed for Throttle Hill. It was him. He was unconscious when I found him."

"Do you think Sam saw who shot him?" Joe said.

"I think so. He probably was so close he couldn't speak into his mike."

"Were there more than one?"

"There had to be. Two of the shots went off almost at the same time."

"What else can you tell us?"

"That's it for now. None of this is for publication, okay?"

Joe and Luke nodded.

Callahan asked Laura if she wanted to talk to reporters. She did not. The sergeant said he would arrange for all press statements to be made by officials at police headquarters.

The double doors into the hall swung open and a short, portly man in green surgical garb approached Laura. He pulled his mask down around his neck.

"Mrs. Roberts, I'm Dr. Hunnicutt." He took the cap off and wiped sweat from a tired, fatherly looking face. "I wish I had better news for you. Your husband took three bullets. One hit the upper left arm—a flesh wound—no problem. But we're having trouble stopping the bleeding where bullets pierced the lower pyloric portion of the stomach and the superior lobe of the right lung. We've got an intertrachial tube in there and . . . well, your husband has a helluva constitution. Anyone else would have been gone by now."

The surgeon asked Laura to stay close—to

be at Sam's bedside if he regained consciousness. Laura said she wouldn't budge from the waiting room.

After Dr. Hunnicutt left, Laura gave about thirty seconds of thought to the doctor's report. Then she turned to the Jays.

"Joe and Jessie, I'm really going to need you in the next few days. So you get some sleep. And you will need someone to help you get ready."

When Luke and Maggie volunteered for the job, Laura said, "Thank you both. Joe and Jessie will tell you what they need. Jessie, your blue nightgown is in the finished pile of laundry on top of the washer. Joe, the new purple and white running shorts you wanted to sleep in are in a paper bag on top of the refrigerator."

I offered to stay overnight with the Jays, but they insisted on staying alone. Arrangements were made for Luke and Maggie to help them get up at 7:00 A.M.

After everyone had left, Laura slumped back on the couch.

"How'm I doing, Barnaby?"

"You look strong from here."

"It's a bluff."

"I'll stay and help you keep it up."

"Stay for a while, please. . . . Help Joe and Jessie keep theirs up, too. Will you?"

"I will, but they look strong, too."

"They're human beings like the rest of us. The only trouble is, they have added problems at a time like this."

"What do you mean?"

"People who don't know them well tend to see them as weaker and less than they are. At other times, they're perceived as superpersons—with special insights and powers. Both views are unfair."

"Laura, I'm one of those misperceiving people. I just hope I can learn fast enough."

"You will."

"How do you know?"

"You have the heart for it. You're not afraid to admit that you're a combination of weaknesses and strengths—like the Roberts and the Jays. . . . But I am worrying about Joe and Jessie. . . . It's just that the stakes are so high for them now. If the pressure becomes more than they can bear . . ." Her eyes became wet. "Everything's blurring together. I feel so overwhelmed."

"Look, Laura. You have just one task tonight: Stay close to Sam. Refer everything else to me. My phone is next to my pillow."

"That helps, Barnaby."

I stayed with Laura until her eyelids began to drop slowly, then rise rapidly like an uncontrolled spring-loaded window shade. I asked a nurse to bring blankets and a pillow, and Laura kicked off her shoes and stretched out. I covered her with a blanket, patted her on the shoulder, and said I'd see her in the morning.

When I got home, the green panel light on my telephone answering machine was glowing. I rewound the tape and turned it on: "Barnaby, it's midnight here in Stanley. Makes it 11:00 there. I'll call back." Click. "Hi, Barnaby . . . still not there, eh? Later." Click. "Barnaby, it's 3:00 here! Have to leave early in the morning. I'll call tomorrow. Hope you haven't decided to replace your old pal Mindy" (nervous laugh). Click.

JULY 5.
AT
6 A.M.
I WAS
OUTSIDE,

ready to walk diagonally across the square to Laura—until I saw Joe and Jessie on the New York-bound train platform. I changed course.

Joe was dressed impeccably—grey slacks, blue blazer, light blue shirt, and navy and white striped tie. Jessie wore navy slacks and a starched cotton blouse, with a gold necklace to top it off. They looked as if they were ready to board the train with the rest of the well-dressed commuters. I studied them silently, then spoke.

"What are you doing?"

"Gathering evidence," Joe spelled.

"Since when?"

"Since the first train."

"You mean the five-fifteen?"

Joe nodded.

"How did you get ready?"

"We helped each other."

As commuters moved onto the platform, Joe and Jessie conducted a quick but thorough visual survey of each one. Not knowing what they were searching for, I leaned back and watched them work.

The six-fifteen pulled up and, like a giant elongated vacuum sweeper, prepared to clean the platform of its passengers. While the Jays studied everyone getting on, I spied an attractive woman in a gray silk pants suit getting off. She had flowing black hair, long thin eyebrows, and a red, well-developed Sophia Loren mouth.

"Mary Ann!" came a shout from a man in a business suit who was preparing to board the train. He left the door and hurried toward the woman. "Mary Ann. It *is* you!"

She threw her arms around his neck. Their lips met and stayed in that juicy position until the conductor called all aboard.

"I didn't know you were back," the woman shouted as the man returned to the train on the run. "I'll call you."

To my surprise, the Jays showed no special interest in her.

"Now that everybody's gone," I said, "please cut me in on what you're looking for."

"We seek a couple of loose pieces," Joe said.

"You'll be the first to know when we find them," Jessie added.

"Fine," I said. "But wouldn't you think that whoever shot Sam would be hiding out just now?"

"No," Joe said. "This organization is so large that Sam's shooting doesn't matter that much."

"It doesn't matter?"

"It was a fluke."

"A fluke?"

"Right. The parking lot is usually empty at night. But last night it was full."

"So?"

"The criminals coming off the trains knew it would be. But they were prepared for patrol cars, not an officer walking a beat."

"Criminals?"

"Yes. And some local people are in it, too."

"From Throttle Hill?"

"Yes."

That sounded far-fetched to me. Sensing my doubt, Joe set his jaw and prepared for the barrage of tough questions I was preparing to ask—until I looked into his eyes. They seemed to be saying, Barnaby, don't question me so much. We must do something. We must keep up the bluff. Don't demean us! Don't break us down!

Joe waited.

"Well, you guys," I said, letting out a long breath. "You two are something else. Go for it. Good luck."

I was so busy looking into their faces, I didn't see Jessie's hands making their way toward mine. Even when she gripped me, I continued to look into the upturned, incorruptible pilgrim countenances of two persons committed to being the very best people they could be.

And this time, I saw *differences*. Heretofore, the Jays had seemed much the same because I had focused mostly on their wheelchairs and muscular coordination. Now Joe came across as a thinker with a logical, step-by-step mind, a chess player. Jessie, on the other hand, was a free spirit with a repertoire of ready emotions, a girl who would gladly dance on tables.

Laura was right about their communication. Their phrases were refreshingly efficient— clean, clear, concise sentences, always finished, perfect grammar—the kind I struggled to have on paper by the third draft.

But something else made my heart beat faster. I saw a willowy beauty in both of them. It was there, though I knew that curvature of spine and contracture of limbs—disfigurements caused by earlier years without physical therapy—tended to return when they were tired and less conscious of their posture. Their bodies were among the most healthy I had ever seen. Others of the human species would be so much better off if they possessed lean forms like Joe's and Jessie's.

I had always been quick to notice beauty in other human beings—especially women. Now I realized that many of the things that had attracted me were made up of fatty tissue—tissue that in other settings wasn't all that great. For example, I recollected my time with the Fur Tribe in the Sudan. Its members believed that the slightest sign of fat in the buttocks was ugly. They worked hard to keep theirs muscular and flat—which meant they worked harder than most Americans.

And yet, Joe and Jessie had been singled out as not like the rest of us, just because the dispatchers that send messages to their muscles are screwed up, because they have to use wheelchairs, and because they can't swallow spit as well as the rest of us.

With expressive dark eyes, they continued to look at me with kindness and trust, simply because I backed off and refused to chew them up with questions. I felt a sudden urge to wrap my arms around them and hold them tight. Had I really fallen for these two in just four days? Or was I feeling a do-gooder urge that would evaporate after our first fight?

"Well, friends," I said, "how about breakfast at the diner?"

"We have one more commuter to cover," Joe said.

"And then?"

"It will be stake-out time at the parking lot."

"Do you plan to check in at the hospital?"

"We went there earlier," Jessie said.

"You did? How's Sam? How's Laura?"

"Sam's vital signs are better. He is still unconscious. Laura is staying tough."

"Well, you wouldn't mind if Luke and Maggie intercepted you somewhere with something from the diner?"

That brought immediate arm flailing.

I narrowed my eyes and smiled. "You knew I'd offer."

Joe grinned. "We calculated the possibility."

As I headed for the diner, I marveled at Joe's dry humor. But what would he do if Sam died? As I thought about that, it seemed an invisible hand was squeezing my stomach into a sickening tightness. Suddenly I felt jumpy.

Come on, Barnaby, I said to myself. Snap out of it. Don't lose your cool.

At the diner, I got Maureen to roust out Luke and Maggie for food delivery to our detectives. Then I sat down with Postmaster Goodkin and Sean O'Rourke, who were having coffee.

"I called Laura this morning," Maureen told us. "She's strong. Sure hope she can last. . . . And guess what?"

"What?"

"Laura had an early morning surprise visit from Grover Rassmussen."

"Odette wasn't with him?"

"No."

"Good. Without his fascist wife, he's not such a bad guy." I realized my words had sounded acidic, but for some reason it felt good to say them.

Sean mumbled something about Sam being in a coma with slim chances of regaining consciousness. That statement rubbed me the wrong way. I ignored him and changed the subject.

"I'm worried about Joe and Jessie," I said. "I think their bluff is getting thin."

"Better leave them with it," Abe advised. "I think I understand what they're experiencing."

"Since you understand so much, tell me. What are they experiencing?"

Abe, ignoring my sarcasm, did as I requested: "Tell me if I'm projecting my own feelings, but until a few months ago Joe and Jessie lived in a concentration of people with common disabilities. People with various kinds of training were hired to care for them.

Collectively, those people were 'keepers,' and people like Joe and Jessie became the 'keepees.' "

I groaned.

"Now, Barnaby, don't jump to a conclusion! I'm not saying High Ridge is a concentration camp. It certainly isn't. It's just that keepers do possess the power to set rules about how the keepees shall live. It could be a good power, and keepers can develop humane rules.

"But here are two young people who suddenly have a chance to be their own keepers—to take control of their own lives. And you, Mr. World Improver, responded true to form. You may not have understood what was going on in their heads, but you caught their spirit."

"Did you ask me to tell you if you were projecting your own feelings?" I inquired.

"Yes."

"You are."

Abe leaned forward as if he were trying to see what was going on behind my eyes.

"Barnaby. *Barnaby.* It would be tough, going back to High Ridge. It would be like winning ten million in the New York lottery, and then having the judges say they made a mistake. Forget that!—You're not a materialist. Just assume that . . . that Mindy pulled out of your life."

"Cut it out, Abe," I said. "What's all this grim back-to-High-Ridge baloney? What's the matter with all of you? Sam is still alive. Nobody is going back to High Ridge. And by the way, Mindy is okay . . . even though I missed a telephone visit with her last night."

Abe paused, then took a sip from his cup but kept his eyes on me. "Barnaby, my friend . . . don't mess up when it comes to that dear woman."

At the counter behind him, Pete and Maureen stood arm in arm, moving their heads up and down like little children, with squinty smiles and pointed fingers.

I took a deep breath and held it, as if an exhalation would splash acid on everybody. I turned to Sean, thinking that maybe—just maybe—he and I would be on the same wavelength for once. No luck. He stared into his cup as if the next ripple in the brown liquid would open to him the true meaning of life.

Still holding my breath, I left without saying so much as a good-bye. I walked slowly around the square until whatever had held my insides so tightly released its grip.

Laura hugged me as soon as I entered the waiting room. "What would I have done without you?" she said.

"You'd still be here, ready to be with Sam at a moment's notice."

"But think of all the supports. We didn't know any of you a week ago."

"Hey, Laura," I said. "Why must everybody be so busy identifying evil forces these days? Is it wrong to believe there are lots of good forces in the world?"

"I should think not, judging by the way you and the others have been sticking with us. Just think. Abe called, said he got my mail from the route man, and he'll be bringing it over. And Luke and Maggie—at first I was worried about Maggie—they've been a great help for Joe and Jessie."

"I heard that even Grover was here."

"Right. Even Grover. I opened my eyes and saw him just sitting in that chair, calmly waiting for me to wake up. He said he was early for his train and wanted to tell me he hoped Sam would be all right. . . . I felt he wanted to say more."

"Maybe he feels bad about the way Odette treated you." When I thought about Odette, my stomach went tight again.

I quickly changed the subject. "Do you need anything?"

"I'm fine, Barnaby."

"I have a phone next to my word processor, too. Call if you need me."

"Thanks, Barnaby."

On the walk back to my place, I saw Odette

coming out her front door, setting herself on collision course with me. I swallowed hard.

"Mr. Shane," she began, "I'm so sorry about that black policeman. He's still unconscious?"

"He is, Odette."

"I knew it. He'll never recover. And now we will have the problem of those two in the wheelchairs."

"What do you mean?"

"Well, did you know they were trying to enroll in the high school?"

"What's wrong with that?"

"They might have fared well if the officer were alive. He'd keep things calm."

"What are you trying to say, Odette?"

"Come now, Mr. Shane. Don't be naive. You know how awful high school students can be. They would eat those children alive, ridiculing and laughing at them! As soon as I heard about it, I went to principal Sparks and told him exactly how I felt."

"You shouldn't have done that, Odette."

"Why?"

"It was unfair."

"You're a fine one to tell me that. *You* come and go. *You've* never been concerned about this community. Those two cripples belong in High Ridge, where they can be happy with their own kind. And those of us who really

98

care about improving Throttle Hill . . . Mr. Shane, I'm still talking to you. How dare you walk away from me! Mr. Shane!"

I had planned to drop in on the gang at the stake-out, but with the tightness building inside me again it seemed wiser to go home and cool down. I once interviewed a man who claimed he wrote poetry to keep from killing people. Suddenly I understood what he meant.

Later when I looked out my window, I saw the stake-out crew had multiplied. There in the bushes were the Jays (still in their best clothes), Luke, Maggie, and three other teenagers. The newcomers were looking over the shoulders of the data-taking Jays with much interest.

The next time I looked, the regular four were moving toward the square on their way to the hospital. The three recruits had been left to run the stake-out.

I wanted to ask the Jays and Luke and Maggie over, but decided against it. Then I felt a sudden urge. I went out to the shed and found a 4 x 8-foot sheet of 3/4-inch plywood and some pieces of 2 x 10 lumber. I went next door and borrowed Jake Bell's portable circular saw. Within the hour, I had cut the ramp floor and angular joists, positioned the pieces, butted it all up to my porch slab, and driven in five times more 16-penny nails than it needed. (Each one was named Odette.) How good it felt to slam those nails!

When I saw the foursome returning, I met them and invited them to my house for soft drinks. Jessie slanted her head in inquiry but decided to accept. Seeing the ramp, Joe made a series of deep-throated sounds.

"That's for sure, Joe," Luke said.

I stopped. "What was that?"

Joe made the same sounds.

I cocked my head.

"Joe said 'Barnaby's place is taking on class,' " Luke translated.

"But he didn't spell it," I said.

"Didn't have to," Luke answered.

Inside, I noticed that Maggie also had caught the knack of comprehending the sounds made by Joe and Jessie—sounds that still made no sense to me. As we talked, the Jays did resort to the boards once in a while with the other teenagers, but not often. With me, always.

"Well, you guys, what does your evidence show?" I asked.

"It's an elaborate operation," Joe reported. "The thieves arrive on the train. Soundview's lot has top preference because it's so easy to get onto I-95 from there. The cars are scouted beforehand. They know which ones they plan to steal."

I had heard Sam say something similar, but I let the Jays pretend they had the facts from amassing hard data. After all, their sleuthing kept them from dwelling on pain that could rip them up inside with the next phone call.

"Good work, you guys. I wish you well."

Jessie made a series of sounds.

I asked her to say them again and she repeated.

Still not decoding, I looked at Maggie.

"She said, 'We still have lots of loose ends.' "

Jessie uttered again and Maggie explained: "We'll need you when we get them together." Jessie punctuated the statement with a serious that's-right nod.

Again it was all I could do to keep from hitting them with a barrage of questions.

"Keep going," I said instead. "But you do need to break from your busy schedule to get out of those dress clothes."

"Good idea," Joe said, and the gang decided to head for Block Five so the Jays could change before returning to the stake-out.

"When you get back, tell the other three to come over for a Coke," I said.

Later, the three rookies appeared at my door: Natalie, with a pudgy round face and blond braided hair, reminded me of a healthy Swiss milkmaid—one of those who wear white starched hats, wooden shoes, and can yodel to neighbors on the next mountainside.

Nicole, petite and slender, had a China doll face and straight black hair that touched her shoulders.

Harley, I recognized as Muscle Shirt, the tall black-haired one who had spirited Maggie away from the picnic. Again he was wearing a purple muscle shirt, out of which protruded unmuscular arms. And again, he reminded me of Don Quixote. But when I got to know him, he turned out to be all right. For example, he arrived carrying Luke's portable radio, blaring "babybabybaby" nonstop. But he turned it off before they entered the house.

Once more I sat quietly and listened to an elaborate description of the stake-out project. I turned on my tell-me-everything-I'm-eager-to-know look (journalists are good at this), though I'd already memorized much of what they were saying.

But as they talked on, I realized that they regarded the Jays as two ordinary teenagers like themselves! They were so busy connecting with the likes, dislikes, and hopes that adolescents hold in common, there was no room to consider disabilities.

As the three left, I looked over toward the

hospital. Don't you dare die now, Sam Roberts, I thought. I have an argument to finish with you. Harley and the two girls had supplied me with fresh evidence that teenagers might—just might—have attitudes that could make a better world. I wanted to corner Sam and tell him that the young aren't constricted by as many prejudices as adults are. Adults will die with prejudices young people will never need to bother with. I felt good as I watched the three return to their stake-out.

But Odette saw them going into the bushes together.

As soon as they were out of sight, she started for the overpass. Surmising what was going on in her mind, I knew I was about to see full-blown adult prejudice in action. With wicked glee, I watched her walk almost on tiptoe as she neared the bushes, her head and shoulders forward.

Then Kevin O'Rourke approached on his bicycle, spied Odette's furtive actions, and stopped. Odette did an about face and walked over to him. I watched her point with ample gestures toward the bushes, with open palms explain the situation, then motion for him to come with her. Kevin stepped back, but she grabbed him by the arm, and they headed for the bushes together just as a train from New York pulled into the station.

From my hilltop, I saw them crash through the bushes into the stake-out. The heads of the teenagers turned away from the train and looked at the intruders as if they were out of their minds. Odette and Kevin, obviously seeing what fools they had made of themselves, left the enclosure rapidly. On the way out, Odette's mouth moved constantly. Kevin tried to get on his bike, but he didn't know how to break away. As he walked his bike toward the overpass, she stayed right with him. At the top of the overpass, I could tell he had had it. He stopped, turned away, spread his feet apart, and gripped the railing with both hands. With his back to her, he stared at the train and the tracks below until she finally gave up and left. Poor Kevin's face was as red as a stop sign, and his chest was heaving as if he'd just finished the hundred-yard dash. Although I didn't often know what was going on in the mind of that shy man, I did this time. I felt sorry for him.

☆　☆　☆

I worked on my book until the end of stake-out time, then decided to take Joe and Jessie to the diner. But when all seven teenagers came out of the bushes, they met three others, and—no doubt about it—they were on their way to McDonald's.

Before they had gone far, Joe and Jessie stopped and spoke to the others. The rest of the gang settled on the curb while the Jays headed for my place. I had the screen door open as they came up the ramp.

"Barnaby, three cars were slated for theft today," Joe announced.

"How'd you learn that?" I asked.

"Three men in suits and attache cases got off a train this afternoon. They took the passageway under the tracks and returned on a train for New York."

"Lots of people miss their stop and have to go back . . . but maybe you are onto something." I tried my best to look serious.

"I *know* I am," Joe insisted. "They were nervous, looking in all directions, and then they got on the train."

"You think they planned to go into the parking lot, grab the cars, and light out of there?"

"Right. Somehow we blew our cover."

I tried to stifle a laugh, but failed.

Joe gave me an odd look.

"Aw, Joe, I'm sorry. But, my gosh, you guys! You run the most sociable stake-outs I've ever seen! Kids going in and out . . . "

Jessie swung her wheelchair sideways at my leg and gave me a beseeching look. "*We* want friends, too."

Silence. Then the fear and strain she had been trying so valiantly to keep under control began to show in her eyes as she looked up at me.

"Aw, Jessie. . . . What's the matter with me? . . . I'm proud of you. . . . You're doing fine."

More silence. I thought I saw a tear coming from little Miss Emotions. Before it fell, though, she glanced at Mr. Calm Thinker. When she looked at me again, it was gone.

Joe continued as if there had been no interruption. "Barnaby, local people are involved. They spot the types of cars the crooks want and signal when the coast is clear."

I nodded as if I were hearing that for the first time. "You may be right, Joe. What do the other kids think?"

"We can't tell them."

"Why?"

"They've lived around here too long. They wouldn't believe us."

"When we find out who it is," Jessie instructed, "*you* will speak to the authorities for us."

Our confidential session over, they wheeled back to their friends. The Jays looked as together and purposeful as ever. Even so, I sensed how precarious their situation really was. It was as if they cautiously carried within them the knowledge of Sam's uncertain condition as one might carry a handful of razor blades. As long as Sam's future remained in limbo, these two, without a whimper, would maintain the stake-out, confer in a business-like style, and continue their crook-catching scenario as if it were all a glorious challenge. But I shuddered when I thought about what would happen if Sam died.

I
WATCHED
THE
JAYS
AND
THEIR
RETINUE

enter McDonald's on the other side of the square. Not wanting to work anymore, I leaned back in my chair and spied John Hawke's newsclips—the ones I had been shoving aside for the past few days. Tearing open the envelope, I read each story my journalist friend had wanted me to read earlier. . . . Then I read them again. Although I'm no mystic, I felt I was reading them at exactly the right time.

Later, I took off for the hospital. As I walked, I recalled my jumpiness in the diner, the strain in Jessie's eyes. I knew Laura must be close to the breaking point, too. How long could she hang on?

When I got to the waiting room, I found Grover with Laura again. He got up.

"Hi, Barnaby," he said. "I simply had to drop in before I went home."

He cast an uneasy glance at the door, as if Odette were about to appear and eat him up. "I'd better go now . . . but I had to see how Officer Roberts was doing."

"It was kind of you to stop in, Mr. Rassmussen," Laura said.

"I'll see you again, Mrs. Roberts. Goodbye, Barnaby."

I slanted my head in inquiry when he was gone.

"He was nice," Laura said. "I think he feels bad because his wife has been so hard on the Jays, and he wants to make up for it. When I told him Sam would be transferred to a room where I could stay with him, he offered to relieve me. He insisted he could take a later train in the morning or an earlier train home."

"Great, but what was that about Sam?"

"The doctor says he's still in a coma, but the internal hemorrhaging has stopped. Tomorrow morning he will be in a room two doors down the hall."

Laura flopped back, let both hands fall limply to the couch, and breathed a sigh.

"How do I look now, Barnaby?"

"You look like a propped-up Raggedy Ann doll—but a nice one."

"Dr. Hunnicutt said I shouldn't get my hopes too high. He said that if the bleeding starts again . . . well, in Sam's weakened condition, it could be over."

I nodded slowly.

"It's getting harder to laugh," she said.

"No kidding."

My irony touched her just right. A tiny chuckle came out like a cough. "You're a comfort, Barnaby."

"That's what you get for letting me crash into your kids."

"That crashing paid off. Pete and Maureen keep showing up with meals and snacks, the O'Rourkes bring me newspapers and magazines, and our gentle postmaster is here every other hour with bits of fatherly advice. And then there's the Jays' growing honor guard of teenagers."

"Those kids are something else. God help Soundview High School if the Jays are enrolled! Remember how Tom Sawyer convinced his friends it was a high privilege to take over his job of whitewashing the fence? Well, he couldn't hold a candle to your two. Don't be surprised if someday the Jays lead the Soundview High band down the middle of Front Street."

"That would be the day. But where are all the heartless ones—the sneering kids who can give the Jays a hard time?"

"They're out there. The Jays have just been lucky so far."

Silence.

"Hey, Laura. Is all this talk helping?"

"Barnaby, don't stop talking. Talk about anything—shoes, ships, cabbages, kings, as Alice in Wonderland said—anything. If I lose my ability to talk freely, I . . . "

"Okay. Get this: Luke and Maggie can understand some of what Joe and Jessie are saying."

"I know. Harley is getting the knack, too."

"Can you do it?" I asked.

"Not that well yet. Why some people can and others can't remains a mystery. Maybe some people are more sensitive to eye and lip movements. And maybe as we grow older, we don't hear the highest and lowest frequencies so well.

"You know, there was an elderly Englishman with cerebral palsy—Joseph John Deacon. His three lifelong friends helped him write a book about his life in an institution. His friend Ernie Roberts was the only one who knew what Mr. Deacon was saying. Like Luke, he translated to a second man who wrote the sentences in longhand, while the last man typed it. Roberts, the interpreter, often traveled with Deacon."

"That haunts me."

"Why?"

I told Laura about John Hawke's newsclips. He had written about Anne McDonald, a nineteen-year-old with cerebral palsy who had spent sixteen years wasting away in cribs and beanbag chairs in a Melbourne institution. She had been diagnosed as profoundly retarded, incapable of communicating with any other human being.

Then came Rosemary Crossley—a new-breed teacher like Laura—who taught Anne to communicate on a board, as the Jays did. Rosemary found Anne to be highly intelligent. But when she took the good news to the superintendent, a physician, he refused to believe that Anne's only trouble was athetosis, a severe muscle problem.

Rosemary was ordered to back off, but she didn't. Eventually she was fired, but she continued to fight for Anne, all the way to the Supreme Court. In the hearings, the physicians were split. Half said Anne possessed little or no intelligence. The others maintained she had only cerebral palsy and was intelligent. Complicating the case, Annie's muscles would cramp under pressure—especially in front of those who were out to prove she lacked a mind.

Finally, the judge took Anne into another

room. For fifteen minutes, he relaxed with her. Then he gave her two words to spell on her communication board for her teacher—*string* and *quince*—two words that only she and he knew. The judge came out and told Rosemary to go into the room with Anne. After she was gone, the judge told the audience what the two words were, and they waited to see whether Anne could spell the words for Rosemary.

When Rosemary came out and spoke the two words Annie had spelled, the courtroom broke into laughter—partly from relief and partly from the teenager's bloodymindedness. She had spelled *string* and *quit*. The misspelling was her way of saying she'd had enough pressure from the court.

Today Annie lives with her teacher in Melbourne. She has co-authored a book and attends classes at a university.

Laura said, "Barnaby, bring me all of Mr. Hawke's newsclips. First thing tomorrow." Then she began to talk enthusiastically. She told me this sort of thing was happening all over the world.

When I marveled at the value of communication boards, she said that was only the beginning—a number of new things were being introduced in the computer age. She described remote-control devices that could be activated by the slightest body movement—focusing the eye, moving an eyelid, tilting the head, controlling the breathing, and even by controlling blood-pressure changes. These devices would enable people to dial telephones, voice words through a speaker, correct posture, set special-function robots into motion—even fly airplanes, gliders, and hot air balloons, or drive cars. Laura was still talking about such breakthroughs when the Jays arrived with their friends at 9:00 P.M. Then she shifted gears to the thoughtful mother. She made certain Joe's and Jessie's evening arrangements were set. She calmly listened to another reiteration that there would be no overnight babysitting for them. She agreed, gave them both hugs, and told them to have a good night's rest. When they left, she resumed her lecture on cerebral palsy, modern technology, and the future.

As the night wore on, Laura's rate of speech slowed and her words became slurred. Then, as on the night before, her eyelids began to flutter. While she continued to talk, I picked up a pillow, fluffed it, and placed it at the end of the couch.

"Laura, lie down." She did.

"Barnaby, don't leave yet."

"I won't."

In her exhaustion, Laura fell into a deep

sleep. But furrows formed on her forehead and her mouth became taut. Again I wondered how long she could handle the strain.

☆   ☆   ☆

When I walked past the Immigrant's Trust Bank, the large red letters told me it was 3:02 A.M. At home, I saw the light glowing on my answering machine.

"Hey, Barnaby," the recorded voice said. "It's Mindy. Where are you? I'll call back." Click. "It's Mindy again. Call me when you get in. Call the international operator and ask her to dial me here in Stanley at (160) 015-5655. I'm stepping up my interview schedule. Maybe I can get home earlier. I leave this morning at 4:00 sharp for East Falkland. You call. It's a tough assignment. I need to hear your voice." Click. "Barnaby? (silence) You're not there yet? (silence) I . . . have to hurry for the plane" (long silence). Click.

JULY 6. MY EYES OPENED AT THE USUAL TIME AND THEN CLOSED.

11

I rolled onto my side, snugged the covers under my chin and felt myself slipping back into heavenly sleep. Then I heard wheelchairs whizzing up the ramp. I dragged myself out of bed and to the door.

"Barnaby, Sam's in trouble," Joe said, his hands moving emphatically over his communication board.

"What?"

"We're sure Sam knows who the local crooks are," Joe said.

"So?" I commented sleepily, not reminding them that Sergeant Callahan had said something to that effect earlier.

"He needs police protection! Please ask for a guard!"

Not wanting to involve Callahan in the Jays' busy illusions, I let their request hang and waited for them to say something else.

"Will you?"

"Okay, I'll call the station."

"Thanks."

They hurried back to their surveillance post.

Since Callahan was duty sergeant for the evening shift, I didn't want to wake him up. I went to the diner for breakfast before telephoning. On the way, I stopped in at O'Rourke's and bought the *New York Times* from Sean.

"That was nice of you and Kevin, taking newspapers and magazines to Laura." I spoke as softly and carefully as I could.

"Glad to. Nice lady," Sean said. He seemed more talkative than usual.

"She is. Nice kids, too. They think they've almost cracked the case."

"They have?" His blue eyes widened. His expression showed a healthy interest.

"Not really. It's just their way of handling things. They keep a daily ritual of stake-outs. Now they tell me some locals are involved."

"People on Throttle Hill?"

"You got it. They have license numbers and makes of cars, identifications of people and their movements that would amaze you. If someone local were a crook, they'd have the evidence by now. They'd only need time to piece it all together." I laughed.

Sean gave a quiet laugh.

As I headed for the diner, I heard a throaty sound. It was Joe on the station platform. I walked through the passageway between O'Rourke's and Vittorio's and up the ramp. Joe took me to the south end where we could talk in private.

"There could be bloodshed around here soon," he said.

"You're kidding."

"No. This organization is so big it could wipe out everyone who knows about them."

"Now, Joe. Who would they wipe out?"

"Sam, me, Jessie, you—because you've been seen with us—and the local hoods."

"Aw, Joe. Aren't you getting carried—"

"Did you call Sergeant Callahan?"

"Not yet."

Joe tapped me lightly on the side of the leg. "Please."

"I'll call from the diner."

Joe headed back to Jessie.

In the diner, a businessman stood at the phone, the handset clamped between his shoulder and ear while he made notations on a clipboard. I sat down with Abe and Kevin and ordered Vittorio's "Big Breakfast." When Grover came in for coffee, I invited him to join us. He did, and I could tell he felt comfortable with us.

"How're the detectives?" Maureen asked as she reached our table with plates balanced on an arm.

"Busy and wild."

"What do you mean?"

"Joe thinks there's going to be bloodshed. The big bad thugs from the city will descend on us any minute. They'll wipe out the Jays, Sam, all their spotters in town, and even me."

"And not the other teenagers?" Abe asked.

"No. Joe shares his bottom-line conclusions only with me. The kids hang around more as friends and workhorses."

"The jig's up, honey," Pete said, coming up beside Maureen. "We've had such a good front, I never thought they'd catch us."

We all laughed—all except Abe. "Maybe we should listen to Joe."

"C'mon, Abe," I protested, "those two have wild imaginations. They've created this monstrous system in their minds."

"They've survived some monstrous systems before. Give them credit for that."

"Abe, I know where you're coming from. But can't you see that the Jays are forcing themselves into busy work? It's just an emotional exercise."

"You may be right. I'm not as close to them as you are, but I've watched them getting around

119

like overactive vacuum cleaners. They're fighting to survive as citizens of this town."

"What's that got to do with crooks?"

"They must keep their eye on anything that threatens to do them in."

"But look at the hopeful side," I said. "Look at the great support system that has emerged around them—the Roberts, me, all of you, the young people."

Abe laughed. "The way you look at the hopeful side—who else needs to look?" He stretched out his hands, palms up. "That's why we click—you with your head in the clouds looking for saints, and mine close to the ground, smelling for devils I can tiptoe around, or attack, if I have to. Together we make a fuller picture. So listen to them when they get fearful. What's to lose?"

"But Joe wants me to bother Sergeant Callahan. He wants me to call him and—"

Abe placed his hand on my arm. "Bother him."

The businessman still had the phone tied up. I went home to use my own.

Callahan was already at work and, to my surprise, he said he'd be delighted to meet with Joe. He suggested Vittorio's Diner and asked if he could bring a few of Sam's fellow officers with him. They could be there in fifteen minutes.

I went to tell Joe. I had started across Soundview Avenue when a small man in work clothes and steel-toed oxfords approached. His strides were long and sprightly, and his arms swung like pendulums, though one hand gripped an old-fashioned, pyramid-shaped overnight bag. He had to be seventy, but his sinewy build and short, silvery hair gave him the appearance of a pocket-sized Spencer Tracy.

Our eyes met.

"Well, the Yanks got tromped last night," he remarked.

"The Yanks?" I asked, a little surprised at the way he opened up to a total stranger.

"Right—the Yankees got creamed. It was beautiful. Cal Ripken got four for four. And good ole Freddie Lynn started for the first time since he broke his ankle. Eddie Murray got two homers. Ya know what? Now that Earl Weaver's back as manager, things're gonna pull together."

"You were there?"

"Sure was. Took the train up from Baltimore."

"I had planned to be at that game."

"Ya had? Well, if yer a Yank fan, you would of been sick."

"You sound like a real Baltimore booster."

"Sure am. Ever since I was a little kid. When Aggie and I had a daughter, we even named her Oriole. She lives here. Maybe you know her. Oriole Rassmussen?"

"Odette?"

"Heck no, nothing fancy like that. *Oriole*. She's lived up here a little under two years. We . . . well, we had a falling out. And since I took the train up to the Big Apple, I thought I'd come up and try to patch things up. Ya see—by the way, I'm Ephraim Stransky." He held out his hand.

"I'm Barnaby Shane."

"Real glad to know ya, Barnaby. I own the Stransky Septic Tank Service. Darned good business. Got six tank trucks, goin' all the time. And when Oriole married Grover, I took him on as my bookkeeper. Only thing, me and my men were working harder and harder, but the profits were gettin' smaller and smaller. It took six years before I saw how that little crook had been cleaning us out. He had one helluva leeching system going. Of course, Oriole was tied up in the scam, too. When I finally caught 'em, everything blew up. But then Oriole inherited a big chunk of money from an aunt, and they moved to Soundview."

"Grover Rassmussen is a successful manaager in a New York bank now."

"You kiddin'? He's a rinkydink teller. I got

a guy keepin' tabs on him. And if he's successful, he must be makin' out again like Jason and the Argonauts—out to fleece somebody."

My heart skipped a beat, then pounded as if it would burst through my chest. I looked over his shoulder at Joe and Jessie, and wanted to run to them. But he kept talking, and I had to hear more.

"I couldn't prosecute. After all, Oriole's my only kid, and now I've had some time to think. Oriole had it tough at school, what with all the kids teasing her for being the daughter of a 'honey dipper,' and names worse than that. Aggie and me, we tried to make up for it by treating her like a princess, but the more we did for her, the more she treated us like we was peasants. . . . Well, whadda ya know. Here she comes now. Hi, Oriole."

Odette charged her father, her face the color of my tigerlilies, her eyes like a snake's preparing to strike. She grabbed him by the arm and jerked him so hard he nearly fell down. She pulled him up.

"What are you doing here?" Her harsh voice snapped out the words. "What have you been telling him?"

Odette locked both hands on one of Mr. Stransky's arms and ran backward, pulling him. He staggered twice, but she hauled him up again and kept dragging him toward her house.

Just then I saw Sergeant Callahan drive up to Vittorio's. A second patrol car pulled up alongside Callahan's and three officers followed him inside. Controlling a wild urge to dash for the diner, I strolled slowly in that direction as if nothing were wrong.

"Do you have the time, sir?" It was an athletic looking, middle-aged man wearing a gray suit and vest, coming up from behind, taking long strides and swinging a rich looking attache case.

I stopped. "It's six after seven."

"Thank you. Now I must tell you that your friends are dead, sir, if you fail to do what I say."

His attitude and diction were so proper that his words didn't sink in right away. I looked at the sharp crease of a freshly pressed suit, a glistening white starched collar, the subdued gray and white striped necktie, and I smelled the fresh application of aftershave. This guy looked and sounded like all the others whose wives kissed them and pushed them out of the house in time to make the train—until I looked into his eyes, deepset and squinting—killer eyes.

"Look at your friends, sir."

Moving toward the south end of the platform, away from the huddle of commuters, were Joe and Jessie, their heads swiveled in my direction. Two men in business suits walked beside them, showing interest, talking to them. Joe stopped his chair, and one of the men put a "kind" hand on his shoulder, grasped the wheelchair's control with his other, and moved the chair forward. When they reached the end of the platform, an amiable-looking conclave took place, the men doing the talking.

"They know a wrong move from them will spell your end," the man said. "And if anyone gets curious about those two men, they are social workers from High Ridge who have dropped in for a follow-up visit. The hour is unorthodox but justified, since field personnel are en route to the institution for a special meeting. There are more of us, Mr. Shane."

"But why?"

"See us as repairmen, Mr. Shane, who seek to mend a gap in our services. But first we must survey the damage. You three and some others have information."

"Other teenagers have it, too."

"One of our agents tells us they don't."

"The officers in the diner know."

"They would have known, had we not drawn this circle of containment. As you can see, we are precision people."

"What do you want from me?"

"First, stop looking as if you're about to have a stroke. Relax. Face me. Look interested as I talk. . . . That's better. Walk as close as you can to the front of the postoffice and the news store, turn right, and go onto the train platform. Lose yourself in the crowd. The seven-fifteen arrives in five minutes. Take the first seat in the first car, just to the left of the motorman's cubicle." He handed me a ticket. "Get off at Sterling."

Sterling was the next stop, six minutes away.

"What if the police come out?"

"You will avoid them."

"How?"

"Tell them Mr. Hill and Mr. Johnson from High Ridge have come to visit the two young people and Mrs. Roberts at the hospital and that you will call as soon as they leave. As you can see, the commuter crowd now extends to the walkway between the buildings. I will stand behind you."

"If your men and the Jays are going over to the hospital, why don't you let me join them?"

"Mr. Shane. Please. You now have four minutes. Move."

I went toward the platform, Gray Suit at my side until he casually dropped behind me as I mingled with the crowd. I worked my way south until I stood where the first car would stop. Twenty yards separated me from the Jays. They sat rigidly in their chairs, staring straight at me. The man with his arm around Joe was looking kind and speaking into his ear. The other man was down on one knee, talking to Jessie.

I could guess the plan. As soon as I was on the train, the Jays and their captors would go to the ramp on the north end of the platform and along the far side of the square to the hospital.

The seven-fifteen arrived. All seats were taken in the first car, but as I approached the front seat next to the motorman's cubicle, a man in three-piece brown got up, smiled, and signaled.

"Take my seat, sir. I'm getting off at the next stop." Again I looked into a face of civility, with eyes that failed to match. As I settled down, I could look out the window at Joe, Jessie, and the two men up ahead on the platform.

I wanted to kick myself for being so easy for Gray Suit. I should have refused to get on this train. I tried to stand, but Brown Suit was beside me, a palpable threat.

The platform was almost empty.

"Next stop—Sterling," the conductor announced over the loud speaker. "This train will then express to 125th Street and Grand Central Station. All aboard."

The doors closed. Looking out the window, I saw the crooks inching Joe and Jessie along the platform. Joe balked again, but his man skillfully activated the control.

As they came closer, the Jays spied me in the front seat and our eyes met.

The train began to move.

While the two men continued to look like helping professionals, jabbering niceties, Jessie suddenly jammed her control full-speed ahead, hung a sharp right, and plummeted off the platform. The heavy chair dropped five feet and hit the first set of tracks with a terrible crunch, catapulting her through the air. She landed spread-eagled, face down on the inner high-speed tracks. She didn't move.

The motorman hit his emergency brakes and stopped.

The "social workers" looked at each other, then walked away. Brown Suit, my captor, retreated through the rear door into the second car.

Then I heard the distant shrill whistle of the fast Boston to New York AMTRAK, tearing toward us on the inner tracks.

Joe heard it, too. He took off through the air in his wheelchair, crashed, bumped, and hurtled toward Jessie. He worked an arm over her and I saw him screaming into her ear, trying to pull her off the track. Jessie was unconscious. Joe yelled again. The AMTRAK whistle blew louder, closer.

I jumped into the aisle, banged on the motorman's cubicle.

"For God's sake, open the passenger door!" I shouted. I ran to the outlet at the middle of the car and plunged out just as the two panels slid open. But as I ran toward the front of the train, I heard the deafening sound of the AMTRAK's engines, the clacking of wheels, and the now constantly shrieking whistle as it passed.

I stopped and prepared myself to bear the sight of carnage. Lord knows I'd seen bloodshed before, but it had never been related to people who meant as much to me as the Jays. My throat felt as if a golf ball were stuck in it. I swallowed hard and walked on, almost at a crawl. When I came to the front of the commuter, I saw Luke sitting cross-legged on the outer tracks with Jessie, still unconscious, cradled in his arms. Harley sat beside him holding Joe, who was reaching over, hanging onto Jessie with both hands.

IT IS LABOR DAY MORNING AND I AM ALONE

on Lookout Ledge. The days are getting shorter. I'm waiting to watch the sun rise one last time before leaving on an assignment. There's a slim chance that any of my friends will join me here this morning. They're sleeping off a delightful party that lasted until the wee hours. I would have slept in, too, but this was my last chance to sort out the happenings of those five explosive days in July.

During the rest of the summer I have tried to find adequate words to express the way I felt about those few seconds that separated the dying and living of Joe and Jessie.

Luke, knowing the Jays would be on watch alone, had overcome his adolescent propensity for sleep and had called Harley, Maggie, Natalie, and Nicole. Of course, women take longer than men to get ready, so Harley and

Luke were just crossing Soundview Avenue onto Front Street when they saw Jessie go over the side. I was rushing to the door of the train while Luke and Harley were sprinting toward the platform. They climbed up, ran across, and leaped onto the tracks.

Jessie regained consciousness while she was still in Luke's arms. A black and blue knot the size of a baseball was puffing on her forehead. The whole right side of Joe's face looked as if he'd been smacked with a two by six. Yet neither had a broken bone.

When Callahan and the officers arrived, I told them to get protection to Sam, fast. The morning air reverberated with sirens, converging on the hospital. Actually, the crooks didn't make an attempt on Sam's life. Once Jessie had broken their "circle of containment," it would have been futile to silence Sam. Instead, an uncertain number of "precision people" suddenly vanished.

That night Sam opened his eyes, saw Laura, smiled feebly, and mumbled something about nothing ever stopping him from making Chief. Then he drifted off, slept fifteen more hours, and from that time on, improved. He attended our special event last night, making a third in the wheelchair brigade. Dr. Hunnicutt said it would take time for his wounds to heal, but he should be back in uniform by Thanksgiving.

Abe made a big deal about Sam, Joe, and Jessie now being members in full standing of a glorious fellowship of "survivors," a special group that possesses an uncanny knack for seeing a richness in life that others can never see.

Shortly after Luke and Harley had pulled the Jays to safety, Odette and Mr. Stransky showed up on the platform, and I screamed to Callahan to arrest her. But Joe began waving wildly and making loud sounds.

"The real crooks are in our stake-out," Luke translated. Callahan, now willing to believe anything Joe said, called for help and ordered the area surrounded. Policemen closed in with drawn guns.

The red-faced O'Rourke twins came out of the bushes with hands raised as high as they could get them and eyes bulging with fear.

They screamed, "We give up! Don't shoot!" again and again. Later they delivered full confessions, telling how they had received an easy $500 for every scouted car. An agent from the organization made daily stops, purchased a paper, and left a list of sought-after autos. One of the twins would bike through the parking lot, eye a columbine blue Continental sedan, bordeau burgundy Porsche coupe, or some other specified color and make. After calling in their finds, one of them arranged to be on the railroad overpass when the thieves arrived on a midday train. He would signal "all clear" by hunching down and leaning on the railing with both elbows, looking like an innocent train watcher. But if someone were in the lot or a patrol car approached, the twin would raise up, spread his feet apart, and grip the railing with both hands.

The organization knew the parking lot would be packed on the evening of July 4 and had notified the twins that their hirelings were coming for random picking. At the appointed time, relying only on street lights, Kevin was on the overpass, giving the all-clear. When Sean closed the store at 10:00, he saw Sam going through the passageway under the tracks toward the parking lot. He ran after him, calling, and Sam turned back, but too late. He was ambushed from three directions. Since fireworks were exploding everywhere, no one was the wiser.

Actually, I had activated what was almost Bloodshed Day when I bought the paper and blabbed to Sean about the Jays' data taking. As soon as I left, Sean called the organization and begged them to lay off for a while. But the organization had other ideas. They sent their "precision people" to Throttle Hill as fast as they could.

Then on my way to the diner, Joe had called me aside and told me that local people would be targets. I mentioned that fact facetiously at breakfast, in Kevin's presence, and he had hurried to tell Sean. Quickly they locked their store and went out the back way through the tunnel under the tracks. Crouching between cars, they had crossed the parking lot and sought refuge in the Jays' stake-out. Joe had seen them making their curious retreat.

The O'Rourkes, never dreaming their easy-money affiliation could lead to attempted murder, had plea-bargained, describing two of the contact persons who came regularly into the store. But before the men could be arrested they were found alongside a country road, hands tied behind them, their bodies riddled by bullets.

This secondary "circle of containment" has enabled the mob to continue their method of filling cargo holds and chop shops with stolen automobiles, and cars continue to be stolen from parking lots up and down I-95—except from the Throttle Hill lot.

The presence of twenty or more teenagers —trained by the Jays, who schedule their assignments to the stake-out or the train platform—has reduced thefts to absolute zero, saving the township an estimated $780,000 in stolen vehicles.

Although I never understood the reason for the early morning surveillance of commuters, that bore fruit, too. The Jays solved what they called The Case of the Diamond Spitters. After taking time and description data on three situations in which a man and a woman met each other with exuberant surprise and long juicy kisses, they notified Sergeant Callahan. Together, they broke a million-dollar, mouth-to-mouth diamond smuggling ring. Later, Joe and Jessie recounted with glee the arrest and the twenty-four-hour delay in recovering the stolen merchandise. When the officers closed in, the recipient had swallowed the evidence.

On the afternoon of what could have been Bloodshed Day, Odette had come to my door.

"Papa told you everything?" she said.

"He did, Odette."

"Did you tell anyone else?"

"No."

"Will you?"

"I don't want to hurt *you* . . . but I don't want my *friends* hurt, either."

For a moment, Odette's eyes went glassy, as though her brain might suddenly have been wrenched. She left without a word.

The next week, more than twenty kids and Odette—that's right, Odette—surprised the principal of the high school in his office. They presented a paper that listed thirty-four reasons why the Jays should be enrolled. They also added sixteen planned interventions when needed—including side-by-side translating to the teacher when oral answers were required, transportation assistance, mealtime help in the lunchroom, one-to-one tutoring when needed, and on-the-spot advocacy when unforeseen prejudicial situations might arise. This last intervention, according to Luke, could include actions ranging from a thoughtful appeal for fair play to a therapeutically beamed fist. They accentuated their plan by telling the principal they were "precision people." How it happened I still don't know, but Odette had served as summarizer for the task force.

I privately attributed Odette's transformation to my own silence. But I was wrong. I heard later that Grover had come home that evening with new fire in his eyes.

"You never like what you already have in life, and you never stop shoving me to get you something you don't have," he had shouted, with Ephraim Stransky present. "No more! I quit! I'm leaving!"

Odette had gone into hysterics as Grover threw clothes into a suitcase. Finally, she screamed that she needed him and asked what she could do to make things right. He had a ready answer: Take $11,234.07—the exact amount she had pressured Grover to embezzle from the Stransky Septic Tank Service—out of the inheritance money she had received from the aunt and give it to her father.

She wrote out the check on the spot.

After that came many delightful curbside conversations with Ephraim, the Oriole lover. On mornings after Baltimore played in New York, he would arrive in town, seek me out, and give me the latest on Weaver, Ripken, and Lynn. Then he would launch into his recollection of Grover confronting Odette. You could tell from the stars in Stransky's eyes that he held that feat right up there with clutch hits by Babe Ruth, Lou Gehrig, Pete Rose, and Ty Cobb.

Luke, Maggie, and the gang have succeeded in their ruthless pollution of the Jays' taste in music. Four times this summer, Joe and Jessie transferred to their fold-up wheelchairs and traveled with the others to New York to be hopelessly corrupted by rock concerts. Now even they fake retching with the rest when I bring up "Sentimental Journey."

Last night there was a wedding at my house—mine and Mindy Guthrie's. I'm still not completely sure how it came about. First there was my unexplained unavailability whenever she called. Then came some garbled communications, via transoceanic phone, that I had been spending long evenings with a woman named Laura. Finally Mindy shortened her return date to the first of August.

When she arrived, we spent a week shouting at each other. When we finally tried to be rational, we hurled phrases like "I need an emotional partner," "You have to accept me exactly as I am," and "If we do it, we begin a punishment or reward system" at each other. Then we made the leap.

Joe served as my best man and Jessie was Mindy's maid of honor. The decision to have them "stand" with us came naturally. Those two unwitting catalysts had forced Mindy and me to look at each other in a new light. Also, Mindy quickly fell in love with them after seeing them mirrored in my eyes.

Oh yes, we also offered to pay the Jays back by standing up for them if and when, as adults, they decided to take the big step.

Mindy and I leave for Australia this evening. We plan to write as a team. First we'll cover Australia's attempt to keep the French government from carrying out nuclear tests in the South Pacific. Then we'll report on the preparation for defense of the America's Cup. We've never worked together before; we could end up in more shouting matches. If we do, I will head for Canberra, Auckland, and the Mururoa Atoll in French Polynesia to cover the nuclear thing while Mindy goes to Perth for the sailing scene. So we have an alternative plan, although we hope we click as collaborators.

And the Jays and the Roberts have insisted we spend some time with the Supreme Court winner Anne McDonald and her friend and teacher, Rosemary Crossley. John Hawke, my journalist friend, has arranged for a visit.

As for the book on how a handful of unlikely people can network together to change a crucial situation for the better . . . well, I wrote this story instead.

The sun has just come up, warming my face, Long Island Sound has just turned as blue as a morning glory's trumpet—and I can hear the whirring of wheelchairs.

"You guys sure don't sleep much."

"You either," Joe said.

We chatted for a while.

Then I said, "Do you want to go back up Soundview Avenue with me?"

"We can't now," Joe said. "Got some data gathering to do."

Silence.

"I'm going to miss you both."

"We'll miss you, too," Jessie said.

Silence.

"Mindy and I will be back."

"Hurry back," Joe said.

I hugged each one—tightly.

More silence.

"Well, I have to tell you, I'm sure glad for that accident back in July."

Joe and Jessie looked at each other and smiled. Then Joe spelled, "What makes you think it was an accident?"

Both went into one of their joyful explosions.

As I jogged away, they were still filling the atmosphere with laughter—a laughter so unabashed and so satisfying, it sounded like music.

THE END